RANTS ON LOVE

RANTS ON LOVE

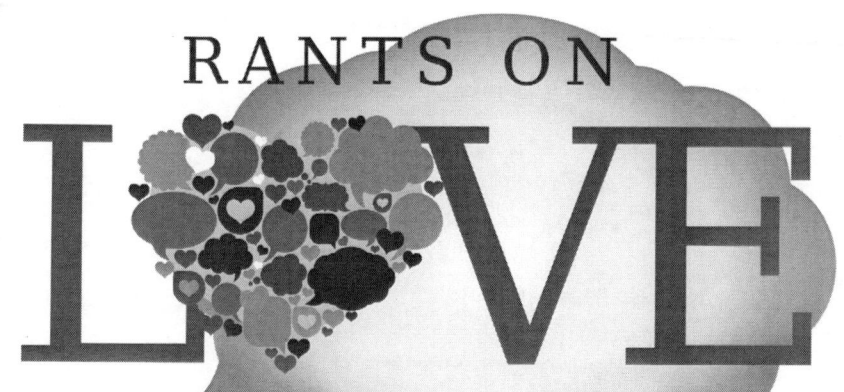

Philosophical Fragments of a Dying Romance

Moses Y. Mikheyev

TATE PUBLISHING
AND ENTERPRISES, LLC

Rants on Love
Copyright © 2013 by Moses Y. Mikheyev. All rights reserved.

No part of this publication may be reproduced, stored in a retrieval system or transmitted in any way by any means, electronic, mechanical, photocopy, recording or otherwise without the prior permission of the author except as provided by USA copyright law.

The opinions expressed by the author are not necessarily those of Tate Publishing, LLC.

Published by Tate Publishing & Enterprises, LLC
127 E. Trade Center Terrace | Mustang, Oklahoma 73064 USA
1.888.361.9473 | www.tatepublishing.com

Tate Publishing is committed to excellence in the publishing industry. The company reflects the philosophy established by the founders, based on Psalm 68:11,
"The Lord gave the word and great was the company of those who published it."

Book design copyright © 2013 by Tate Publishing, LLC. All rights reserved.
Interior design by Gram Telen

Published in the United States of America

ISBN: 978-1-62994-675-7
1. Philosophy / Movements / Existentialism
2. Family & Relationships / Love & Romance
13.11.08

For those who know

"Be very careful if you make a woman cry, because God counts her tears. The woman came out of a man's rib. Not from his feet to be walked on. Not from his head to be superior, but from the side to be equal. Under the arm to be protected, and next to the heart to be loved."

—*An old saying*

ACKNOWLEDGEMENTS

This book is essentially a collection of heartfelt lyrics that would have poured out of my heart had I not strained them into prose. I want to thank all of the people involved in my life who have made this book possible. Søren Kierkegaard oversaw this entire project from beginning to end—he was the extra pair of eyes that I needed when I was writing these rants on a topic so close to Søren's own heart: love. I would also like to thank all of the ladies involved in my life who have somehow—either directly or indirectly—stimulated my thinking. I have been in love with women ever since. I had the pleasure of reading the latest scientific literature on love and also some of the most ancient literature. For this I must thank the English language for allowing me to be exposed to virtually everything ever written on the subject.

I wrote these short "rants" while I was experiencing love. For this reason, they may appear, at times, rather passionate and emotionally-charged. I ask the readers beforehand to forgive my inability, at times, to use more reasonable approaches when dealing with thorny subjects like love. Some of the chapters are journal-like entries, others are conversation-like rants given in the format of a lecture. I have tried to stay reasonably honest in these essays—this means that this book, as a whole, will probably be subject to much criticism. It is inevitable that a passionate subject matter covered passionately would provoke a passionate response. I have written out of love and loss, out of joy and sorrow, out of doubt and faith. This book should serve merely as a conversation stimulator—even if one must pretend that the "discussion leader" (i.e., "me") is insane. I do not see myself as an authority on love; neither do I think that everything I say will apply to everyone for all time. What I deal with is an existential issue: what is love for me? In some ways, this book is very much about me. You, the reader, are bound to either love me or hate me— this all depends on whether you agree with me or not. From my own perspective, I wrote this book in hopes of never publishing it. This book was not intended for you. Moreover, I did not edit this book (excepting the fact that I grazed the pages for grammatical issues). I wrote this as an artifact of my existence. What I had written, I had written. I figured that if I changed something or rephrased it, it would cease to be a genuine historical artifact of my own existence. I decided against editing my works. What you see is what you get.

I would also like to point out that I have changed some of my beliefs since writing this book—these, too, I have not edited. Everything is at your disposal, sift through my writings and see if you can find that paradoxical comment or two; that essay that disagrees with a previous essay; that word that contradicts another. Seek and you shall find. As you read this book, I hope that you drink a lot of coffee and pretend you are listening to a friend ranting. The point is not that you have to agree, the point is that you have to encounter and experience me as an individual. If at some point I disappoint you, you may always feel free to attempt a conversation with me. You could scream at me or shake the book up and down. You could return it. Or maybe you could decide to pass the chapter and read another. You see, friend, there is still freewill even for you out there—choose yourself. In discovering me, you may discover yourself; for we are all human. Pieces of myself I have found in Kierkegaard, Pascal, Jesus, Paul the Apostle, Kant, Aristotle, Plato, Tertullian, Augustine, etc. So can you. I am not asking you to sacrifice yourself for me; rather, I am asking you to listen to the text. Sometimes all another person needs is just to be heard. In hearing the text, you are listening; in listening to the text, you are discovering yourself. In my failures, you may find your own. The log that you see in my eye may be the grenade in yours. The passion I have experienced, you may hijack and use as your own. You see, we are not so different after all.

I would like to thank my friends Roman, Kon and Stan Tochinskiy for allowing me to be a serious person and a complete idiot—sometimes at the same time. I would like to thank my entire family for supporting me and for helping me vent my feelings too. Thanks go to Larisa, Oksana, Julie, Liza, Marianna—my lovely sisters. My brother Elijah also stayed by my side in my darkest moments; he is like a stronghold of stable orthodoxy and moral support. My brother-in-law Ilya Shindyakov was always a good coffee and restaurant companion, along with his wife, my sister, Larisa—thank you for all you do. I would also like to thank Ken Bensiman for being more than just a neighbor but also a genuine friend. I have found a lot of stimulation from my pastor Donald N. Swanson; he is a competent New Testament scholar, theologian, and mentor. He has helped me in more ways than he will ever know.

Jerry Sittser, one of my professors at Whitworth University, has been a good teacher and mentor too. I would like to thank him for instilling in me, and in all of his students, a love of the desert fathers and a love for all of our ancient Christian ancestors. Scott Starbuck, professor of Hebrew and Old Testament at Whitworth and Gonzaga universities, has also been a great influence; he has taught me to love Hebrew and existentialism—in fact, his interpretation of the burning bush event in Exodus 3 is completely existential! (I will have to hijack it sometime!) Last but not least, I want to express thanks to my parents for raising me a Christian. Without them, I may have never met Kierkegaard. And finally, I would like to thank Jesus of Nazareth for showing me what it means to be truly human—in Whom I have found a God worthy to be believed in, honored and loved. May this book serve as a modest and highly flawed contribution to human existential explorations of love.

Contents

Chapter One *Do You Like Coffee?* 13

Chapter Two *The Oscillating Factor: Love And Its Inevitable Rhythms* 26

Chapter Three *The Only Thing Worth Living For Is Love* 40

Chapter Four *The Vainness Of Marital Love: Why Romantic Love Surpasses Marital Love In Passion* 53

Chapter Five *Canned Dating And Other Disposable Inter-Sex Relationships* 61

Chapter Six *How To Know People: An Introduction To Chaos Social Theory, As Presented By A Hardcore Existentialist* 71

Chapter Seven *A Philosophical Look At 'Unconditional Love': The Irrationality Of Such A Love* 76

Chapter Eight *A Flicker Then A Burn* 90

Chapter Nine *Colors* 97

Chapter Ten *Afraid To Love?* 105

Chapter Eleven *Pajamas, Grandmas,
    And Dating Jesus* 110

Chapter Twelve *Questions About Love* 118

Chapter Thirteen *Love Score: How To
    Measure Love* 123

Chapter Fourteen *A Philosophy Of Roses* 133

Chapter Fiveteen *The World In Unity (And Love)* 138

Chapter Sixteen *The Sleeping Lovers* 143

Chapter Seventeen *The Human Motive And Love* 147

Chapter Eighteen *Existentialist Manifesto* 152

Chapter Nineteen *Love, Predestined?* 156

Chapter Twenty *The Contract: How Love
    Conquered Marriage* 171

CHAPTER ONE

Do You Like Coffee?

I am in love. I've been trying to lie to myself for far too long. I have come up with ways to avoid answering these pressing questions which arise in my mind: do you love her? do you care about what happened? I know the answer to all of the questions. She is the answer. Apart from whom I can do nothing. I am bound to her like a tree is bound to the ground it is planted in. I have fallen in love with her at first sight. She will be the death of me.

I met her only once or twice. Briefly. She asked me if I liked a particular philosopher. I replied that I did. She was very inquisitive. I remember thinking to myself that she was the first girl that impressed me—and I am seldom impressed. It was a matter of time before we wrote letters to each other. Love letters. Or so I thought. She was exceedingly beautiful and I was completely knocked off my feet. Never had a woman spoken so boldly! She was vibrant like an early rose in bloom in February, standing out like the sun amidst a starry night. I remember thinking to myself that she was perfect. In fact, I coined the term "perfect" when I met her.

Don't get me wrong, I have always done well with women. The problem that I inherited was two-fold: I fell easily for women and I fell out of love just as easily. Added to this was the fact that I had the intellect to be patient enough to discern the "loves." I was mostly able to distinguish between lust and actual mutual attraction. When she came around, I was left undone. All of my planning was useless. All of my feelings were rent asunder. Nothing mattered anymore. I couldn't find words to say that would help her become my other half. I couldn't find words to create. I was in a state of not being in any state.

After I had attempted to gain her recognition, she quickly pushed me aside. I was relegated to the old dustbin of "insignificant other." I was the Don Juan who was incompetent and unnecessary.

I wrote a writing not to long after that which described my attraction to her quite openly. I wrote it with the notion that she would read it. And she did. She told me that she read it and that she wished to talk to me. I had written essays before and had tried to lure the girl I loved into reading them. She never did—or, I should say, they (plural) never did. I was the Don Juan who attempted to use literature as a means of gaining recognition—I was creating awareness. I used to write lengthy poems. I would call the girl up and leave her a voicemail with a 240 stanza poem (or something like that). The amount of time love consumed! But it was all worth it, even though the women I loved never read a single word I wrote.

It was all useful because hope made all things possible. It was hope that drove me in those days. Hope was my northern star. Hope was my beating heart. Hope was my mother. Hope raised me and turned me into a man. It was hope who clothed me when love ripped my insides out. It was all thanks to hope. I survived.

When she came along, my Mona Lisa, I was torn apart. Love was reckless, it was hopeless for me. I had been burned by the hell fires of love's remains. I had been broken. Simply broken. Nothing was of value anymore. I was in school full-time studying philosophy, theology, and medicine. I was a poet, a musician, a writer. But most importantly of all, I was a *human*.

She could see through my façade. She knew that I was somewhat intelligent and could think my way through things—but knowledge and wisdom is a double-edged sword: I knew beforehand that I would be heart-broken. I knew she wouldn't stay long. Nobody could put up with me. What a venomous mixture is love, philosophy, and theology! She wrung my heart out rightly! She knew what she was doing. She was forsaking me. Plain and simple, she had relegated me to the dustbin of useless existence. I was no longer anything for her; as if I never was anything.

What hurts me the most, even to this day, is that I never had a chance to let her know how I feel. I was hiding behind my artwork. I wrote songs, I published papers, I wrote a book on love and marriage. I was so self-absorbed; I didn't even flinch when she first left. But, oh, I did! She was the only girl that wrote in proper English. I was so adamant about finding someone who wrote me letters *properly*. I have yet to meet a girl who does. She was my one and only, Mona Lisa. I had her.

And I lost her.

This is the funny thing about love and all human relationships: when you obtain something—be it a friend or a lover—you automatically, right then and there, begin focusing your energies and pursuits on something else. The moment the beloved is in your hands, she ceases to be: she is no longer the "beloved"; she becomes the "beheld." It is a sad state to be in. I was there—for the brief being of a sickly and dying moment. I held love in my arms, caressed it—and I had hit it. I had damaged the one thing that was given to me as a precious gift.

Love came to me young, youthful, and restless. She was a pure virgin hoping to be lured. I lured love in and I destroyed it. My hands and my words would betray love. Like Judas Iscariot, I betrayed my savior with my lips and my tongue. My words were written in ink, waxed into paper. It was merely I—the thinking *I*.

This is the problem of my existence. I attempt to act as if everything is a farce. As if life is a play that is being written, and I am the great narrator of it. For so long I have envisioned myself as some sort of Editor too. I was not just the creator and executer of my production, I was the very editor. I could come back and recreate a scene. But that was my delusion. I could not take back my words. I could delete them—but only after I sent them.

I wrote her for days. We had talked about petty things—like coffee, music, and her church-related activities. She asked me what sort of coffee I liked. It seems now, after much reflection, that such a question would be ridiculous and mundane. But it wasn't.

For the objective person who lives by the scientific method, truth is nothing but objective gibberish. But in my world, truth is subjective. Always. You see, though, from an objective perspective, she was stating things that were mundane, from my subjective perspective, her mention of coffee was of utmost and immediate importance. She was now allowing me to speak to her about mundane things. She wasn't bored. I wasn't bored. In my opinion, we were beginning to become mature lovers—lovers who could tolerate and rejoice in the mundane acts of life. I was rejoicing that she chose me as her "coffee companion."

Do you like coffee?

It was such a simple—yet profoundly beautiful—question. I replied yes.

She related how she had tasted a certain coffee brand, which she immediately recommended to me (unfortunately, I forgot the brand as I was unable to find it anywhere).

Looking back at it all, I now know how I had failed miserably. I wish that I could take everything back. I wish that she would write me now and say "Do you like coffee?" I wish she would. I would be prepared to answer her. I would write her a poem about coffee. I would sing her a song about coffee. I would…

I remember being the happiest man alive at that moment. Nothing could take away that sense of oneness and satisfaction from me. My father would ask me to help him—and I would—but it was she who was always on my mind. Whatever it was that I was doing, I was creating a drama in my mind—and she was the most important character. Though I was living in the real world, I had begun to create a world that didn't exist. It was a world which she was in; a world where she and I were star-crossed lovers.

I remember it all too well.

I created a fiction out of a fiction. I created a literature *within* a literature *without* a literature *within* a literature. She was non-existent and yet she was the most important existence of all. I had failed miserably.

Rifts were formed even before I made any errors (that I am aware of). She told me that she had to go to a camp of some sort and that she wouldn't be able to talk to me for a couple of days. Up until that point, I would send her songs that I either wrote or loved. She would listen to my recommendations and dwell in the lyrics. I thought everything was perfect. Except for me. I was never perfect. The storyline was perfect but I, the narrator, had made a number of assumptions. I was creating a story which had an end—but I had not yet even reached the beginning.

She was a very smart girl. There is no reason for me to suppose otherwise. I was the one writing the story anyways—I could insist on the fact that she was, is, and would be smart. I could (and did).

I thought that everything would work out. I needed to come see her. I knew that I needed to become more than just a pen pal of sorts; I could not be some sort of literary creation. I needed to move out of my own storyline and create a reality within the fictional story.

I am not mad or insane. I am human. My existence precedes my essence. I am what I do. My choices are reflections of who I am—and who I am becoming. This story that you are reading is a part of history—because it actually happened—but it is also a fictional construct I created—because it is impossible to verify what actually happened and what caused our separation and essential abandonment of one another. She would probably say that she did not have enough evidence of my existence; that is, she did not spend enough time with me to validate my sincerity and my own existence. She was acting as most girls would act. She knew that if she were to let me come visit her, she would be forced to make a decision. And she was not ready for that. Moreover, she knew that if she were even to invite me to her house, she would already have made a decision: the decision to further our relations to one another in this fictional life. The moment she was forced to make a decision is the moment she lost herself—or, I should say, found herself.

The entire time that we talked, she was living in a vacuum. She was not obligated to make any decisions. We were just two human beings engaging in potential dialogue. She knew that this was harmless and may lead to a potentially satisfying relationship. In other words, it was a win-win situation for her—until I demanded that she make a choice, a decision: allow me to spend historical time with you, I said. She wasn't afraid of living in a literary reality—for it would not hurt anyone (or so she thought). This stream of letters we sent each other—had they been human words, it would have been all the same—were merely creations of our imagination. Our words were literature. Because we were *mostly* words, she had begun to see our relationship as literature. This mean that, like paper, you could edit things out that you didn't really care for. It was here she met someone. Someone more tangible and more real. Someone close by to whom she could relate to.

This was the turning point of our relationship.

This was my magnum opus moment.

I had created a story that was romantic, delightful, funny, beautiful—but not human. I had created a divine literature—I had confused theology for romance.

It was here, at this particular point, that I had my Abraham experience. This is where I, like Soren Kierkegaard, lost my Regina Olsen. This is where I, like Romeo, lost my Juliet. I had given her—the apple of my eye—up to God.

I had decided to return to the one thing that I knew best: theology. I loved philosophy, science, and romance but it was theology which held my heart steady. I knew that I needed to turn to objective truth. I needed more than just story, myth, and Old Testament. I needed a constant, a canon, a rule, a universal absolute.

I needed God.

But I never found Him [sic]. He found me.

In the darkest corners of my heart dwelled love. She was bound in chains—until God showed up. He came unexpectedly, like an uninvited guest. Except He was the one throwing the party. The storyline which I presumably created, was actually just a figment of my imagination: the storyline that I wrote was actually a part of a storyline itself—the divine version, so to speak.

I thought I was the author of this story (and I was). I just failed to realize that God was the Ultimate Editor. My plot was thick, mysterious, and romantic. His plot was...

different. I assumed that she and I were something else. But we were not. It was not to be.

You see, the night I threw everything at God's feet is the night my story vanished. The night I decided to become that Knight of Eternal Resignation, I became an adult. This was the part of my life that was guided by none other than the Greatest Poet of all: God.

I was writing a story within a story—that needed much editing. I simply did not want anybody to change what I had written. Like Pontius Pilate, I had decided to leave the words engraved on the plank as they were.

At this point, I was madly in love. She was the air that I breathed. She was synonymous with the Trinity itself. In fact, she was a part of the Trinity. I loved her. I loved her *as she appeared in my version of the story*. She was a construct of my mind. Something I had created. I had pasted together words and very few actions. Mostly words. I used those words to create a literature which I called by name: Mona Lisa. She was the love of my life. And she did not exist.

I fell in love with someone who existed only for me. She loved me so much that she existed only because I existed. In other words, she only existed because I existed. I created her. My existence presupposed her essence. I created the love of my life. She was nothing but a construct of my own imagination. She was a part of my story. And because she was a part of my story, she was real. She was real *for me*.

I was soaked in tears. The flood gates of my heart were thrust open and destroyed. Like thunder booming from the east, I was overwhelmed by the noise. I had created a romantic Frankenstein that was devouring me from the inside out. I was destroying myself; nay, the story I wrote was taking a vote against me. I was being voted off the island. I, the very author, was being condemned by fictional characters which I created.

God came to me in the night.

I was tired of my own version and I wanted something more tangible. Literature was not enough. As Kierkegaard remarked at one point, in my own paraphrase, it was like reading from a cookbook to a hungry person: it did no good. I was the man who was trying to have literature replace reality. I wanted this girl to be real. But she wasn't. She was only real *for me*. She was not real for God. And that was a problem.

I petitioned God.

I told Him to help me. In the most simplistic manners of all time, He simply answered my prayer. Before I had a chance to even finish my petition, it was answered. I asked God to deliver me from my Frankenstein. But I was not ready to be delivered. I asked God to help me choose. I wanted to be free—I wanted to choose my existence. But I left room for the Editor-in-Chief: God. And that was the wisest choice I had ever made. I asked God for one thing: if she isn't of Your Will, hand her over to someone else; make her fall in love with someone other than me.

I spoke my prayer, went downstairs to my room and found an answer. It was instant messaging from God.

My Mona Lisa—which was a construct of my imagination, a completely subjective truth—was destroyed by another subjectively objective truth: God. God entered the scene as an absolute, a rule, and a canon. He entered the story and it ceased being fictional. It ceased being guesswork. I no longer relied on my ability to reason—for I had no need to. God came in.

The message ran thus: *"I am interested in somebody else right now and do not think that it would be appropriate for me to continue talking to you—and it would not be respectable, on my part, to do that to him. I hope you respect my decision. God bless."*

This was about as divine as a message gets. This was my Abraham moment. I gave up the one thing I loved and gained more in return: I gained reality. It was sad, brutal, harsh, naked, cold but oh-so-real.

The absolute truth, God, stepped into my fictional mind. God, the absolute, stepped into my fictional story, my relative tale. God indigenized so that I would be saved. This was my Jesus Christ moment: God came in the flesh to save me from my flesh. God became fiction so that I could become reality.

I awakened from my wonderful fiction and realized that it wasn't so wonderful. She didn't love me. She didn't even like me. In fact, I never loved her for her either. I loved her as I created her. I loved a figment of my imagination. But with absolutes, all fiction fails.

I still consider myself indebted to her. I do. I believe that if God could save me from myself, so could He save you, whoever you are. This is my story. This is my fiction. This is the tale, the myth which became reality.

Do you like coffee?

CHAPTER TWO

The Oscillating Factor: Love and Its Inevitable Rhythms

It is practically a well-established fact that humans have mood swings. When an ovary-bearing human starts having mood swings, the opposite sex quickly points out that "it must be that time of the month." In other words, humans have taken it for granted that drugs, neurotransmitters, hormones, endorphins, you-name-it, have all been well-known to cause alterations in human behavior. We have known the effects of molecular substances on our character for quite some time now. Give someone something as harmless as coffee in large doses and you end up with a crazed maniac; give someone a peck on the cheek and their heartbeat soars through the roof. (You could have given an IM injection of atropine and the effect would have been similar.) If we all take it for granted that substances "control" us, why have we not taken the logic one step further? Why have we not looked at the conclusive implications of our thinking? For example, if dopamine, a neurotransmitter—a precursor to both norepinephrine (noradrenaline) and epinephrine (adrenaline)—causes, in most of us, generally speaking, an increased heart rate, vasoconstriction (increased blood pressure) and a sort of "high" (happiness), why don't we talk about rhythms and production of the drug? What I mean is this: if dopamine is created in our brain in certain regions and stored in certain definite places, shouldn't we expect it to have a supply-and-demand economy? We know, for example, that dopamine is synthesized by the medulla of the adrenal glands and in the brain by the *substantia nigra*, amongst other places. If dopamine has a direct place of origin and a direct place where it is stored—it is stored in vesicles in axon terminals—we should be able to talk about supply-and-demand more realistically. We know, or hypothesize, that dopamine production is not endless—it is not infinite. You cannot simply have your human body, as limited as it is, produce endless supplies of dopamine. In fact, people with Parkinson's disease have problems with low dopamine levels, they need additional dopamine—which is why they take levodopa carbidopa, a drug that eventually crosses the blood-brain barrier, where it is converted to dopamine. We do not have an endless supply of dopamine—or any other neurotransmitter. What should this tell us? This tells us a few things.

First, if we do not have an endless supply of something, then we must not expect an eternal supply of that something.

In other words, if dopamine is somehow directly related to our general happiness, then logic suggests that that very happiness is not to be expected to be eternal. This means that happiness is not eternal. (And I really don't care what your fiancé told you last night over dinner—once the dopamine runs out, the werewolves come out.) It seems, therefore, that our behavior is very fluid—we attempt to strike a balance between "ourselves" and our hormone-containing bodies—it's a sort of dualism that we are constantly engaging with. If our mood is, at times, however often, affected by "drugs" (such as serotonin, dopamine, oxytocin, melatonin, etc.), it follows that we begin seriously considering "drug cycles," "drug rhythms," and drug economy (supply-and-demand). Let us leave aside this scientific rant for a bit and look at things, as they would appear in the real world, so to speak. Let us look at how the "drug economy" works in real life.

Lily is about to get married. She is a beautiful girl, just shy of twenty-three. She is marrying Mark, a handsome doctor. Lily is extremely excited and exuberant. Mark, too, is having the time of his life. Both of them feel as if things could not get any better. They are madly in love with one another and have to carry around fire extinguishers every single time they have dinner together—too many fireworks shoot out, setting too many fires. They are passionately into each other. Mark writes Lily poems and is recording an album dedicated solely to her. Lily is busy dedicating an Italian dish to Mark. They are hardly ever seen apart in public. When seen, they are always lost in one another's arms. Lily's heart skips a beat every single time Mark even thinks of calling her. Mark, on the other hand, constantly thinks about his soul mate; his mind revolves around Lily like the earth revolves around the sun. Whenever they are together, their pupils are always dilated as large as the moon. They stare at each other constantly. If someone were having a heart attack nearby, they would hardly notice.

Adrenaline (epinephrine) is dopamine's step son, so to speak. Dopamine is, whenever the circumstances require, converted to adrenaline. Adrenaline is released when humans are faced with tough or important decisions. It is responsible for the fight-or-flight response. When a grizzly bear is about to attack us, adrenaline is quickly released. Our heart rate increases. Our lungs take in more air, due to bronchodilation. We are preparing to fight or run. The grizzly is coming closer. The adrenaline causes vasoconstriction; our veins constrict and our blood pressure rises. Perfusion of oxygen into the cells is increased. The blood pressure increases and literally shoves handfuls of oxygen into the cells. Our pupils dilate; they dilate to help us take in as much information and visual data as possible. We want to be able to take everything in. We want to be able to see everything that is coming at us. We want to be able to focus. The grizzly is almost here. And there we are with our pupils dilated as large as the moon, our heart rate soaring through the roof, our lungs taking in large, deep, fast breaths, and our blood pressure is spiked.

We are, essentially, in love.

The grizzly never comes. It was merely a dream. But you get the point.

This is basically what happens when you are in love. Your body prepares for fight or flight. You either ask her out on a date or you run as far away from her as possible. When you come up to that gorgeous girl, your heart rate starts to increase. Of course, first there is a release of adrenaline from the adrenal glands (sitting on top of the kidneys). The closer you come towards her, the more it feels like time slows. Why? Your eyes are now wide, taking everything in. You are more aware of your surroundings. Your brain is, at least in theory, getting more oxygen. The spiked blood pressure is forcing oxygen into the cells. Your brain is processing everything. The way she moves, the way she talks. Her every move is observed and carefully preserved in the cortex and the medial temporal lobe of the brain. Every word she says—no, every syllable—is carefully noted. Where did such acuity come from? Well, thank adrenaline to an extent for that. By the time you reach her, which seems like hours, you already have noticed that she, too, has noticed you—in a good way. Subconsciously, you already know that she likes you. The way she looked at you, the way her pupils were dilated. It was a minute detail, but you caught it. You noticed, be it subconsciously or consciously (if you know this stuff), that her heart rate probably increased and her breathing changed. You noticed how her pupils were soaking in every square inch of you. By the time your hands touch in a friendly gesture, you already made plans for dinner. Love. At. First. Sight. *Absolutely possible.*

Of course, such love is merely made up of the right hormones, endorphins, and neurotransmitters. In fact, if you know a little bit about psychology, sociology, and science, you can probably create love in a test tube, so to speak. All you need are the right ingredients and the right environment. First, you need to relax for a few days before "making" love. You need to let your body replenish all of the stores of dopamine. Second, you set the mood. You make sure the candles are burning just right when you two have dinner. You make sure that the coffee is there too—you will need it. The replenished dopamine will lead the way when the coffee increases heart rate, causes vasoconstriction (increases blood pressure) and dilates her pupils a bit. The low light will also contribute to that. All you need is love, someone once said. Well, I got news: they were wrong. All you need is the right atmosphere, the right lighting, the right mood, and the right neurotransmitters. (Oh, by the way, make sure it is *the right time of the month*!)

Once the atmosphere is right, the pupils dilated aplenty, you can get right down to business. Romance. Humans naturally love dilated pupils. Legend tells us that the infamous seducer, Cleopatra, used atropine.

Why atropine? Well, atropine is similar to epinephrine. It increases heart rate, does some vasoconstriction (increases blood pressure), acts as a bronchodilator, and dilates the pupils. We administer atropine to people who have a heart rate that is almost no heart rate (i.e., bradycardia: decreased heart rate). Cleopatra, for obvious reasons, did not care for all of the scientific jargon and medical uses—she went straight for cosmetic reasons: dilated pupils. Men adore women with dilated pupils. It's the secret ingredient. In fact, many women used atropine eye drops for years, prior to the 21st century. Women in the good old days used atropine whenever they put on eye shadow. Now it has gone somewhat out of style, but maybe we will see a reverse trend after the publication of this writing! Atropine is derived from the plant *Atropa belladonna* (the *Atropa* is thought to be a corruption of the Greek name Atropos, one of the three faiths; the *belladonna* is from the Italian, which means "beautiful lady"). Cleopatra fooled kings, so should you.

But as the night goes on, and once you realize that a lot of this is physiology, you may begin to doubt love. Once you "get the girl," you may begin questioning all of the methods used. Why use something as artificial as candlelight? Couldn't we just "fall in love" without anything material? Without anything like a neurotransmitter? Maybe we can, and we certainly do, but once the neurotransmitters run out, what then?

Rants on Love

Will these feelings last forever?

Back to our first couple. It's great that Lily and Mark are about to get married and that they are madly in love, but I want to ruin the moment. I want us to look at what is going on between the two. We hypothesize (or know) that dopamine is being released in both Lily's and Mark's brains when the two meet. Scientists even think that dopamine might be somehow related to our pleasure and reward system—whenever we do something we like, dopamine is released. In turn, we become happy. We are "rewarded" for doing something we like. If dopamine is being released when Lily and Mark meet, the pressing question now becomes: *when will it run out?* When will the dopamine stores run dry? And when they do, what happens?

This is the most important question. If neurotransmitters are so important in our daily lives, what happens when their stores are run dry? This is the question that I want to now tackle. Because of the inevitable (dopamine, oxytocin, and serotonin do not last forever), we must conclude that—somewhere along the line—the body would respond by sending itself into "restoration" or, more accurately, "replenishing mode." I want to propose a hypothesis, a very modest hypothesis. I want to suggest that our body actually does go into such a "mode." I think that it is very natural to think that way. We must admit that when we run countless miles, we stop to "catch a breath." We all know that. When we run out of dopamine, we, too, I imagine, stop and catch a breath. In that moment, that moment of stopping, we are maintaining homeostasis. We are trying to maintain our survival. Our body realizes that the dopamine is out. The body cannot go on and continue making dopamine at endless rates if you continue to run and waste energy. The body needs to "shutdown" and start replenishing its stores. When we are in a state of euphoria, we must remember, that we are spending countless sleepless nights. We are in a state of absolute catabolism—we are using up and burning up all of our energy and neurotransmitter reserves. When we are "high" we are using up those stores. I think that my hypothesis is modest and rather scientific. One must only look at meth heads. Methamphetamines cause the release of dopamine, norepinephrine, and serotonin, in the brain. They also inhibit the reabsorption of free-circulating dopamine. Basically, the more dopamine and norepinephrine that is freely circulating, the more "high" a person feels. Symptoms include anorexia (you tend not to eat food when you are "high"), weight loss, bronchodilation, vasoconstriction, dilated pupils, etc. Basically, whether you are on meth or in love, you are experiencing the same symptoms.

But here lies the fine print. After meth abuse, there is the inevitable depression that settles in. Deadly and fatal depression. But why? Why, after all of the so-called "good times" and all of the "highs," do people become depressed? I believe that it is *the oscillating factor* that is involved here. What goes up must go down. A release of dopamine must be followed by an inhibition of dopamine excretion and the production of dopamine. The moment you release too much dopamine (you going up) is the moment that is followed by an inhibition of dopamine release and a focus on dopamine production (you going down). The girl that is madly in love finds herself, relatively soon, in depression. The man that madly wants to have sex with someone, finds himself shortly disappointed. One merely must call to mind the biblical account of the obsessive rape of Tamar by Amnon (2 Sam. 13), which was followed by absolute hate and repulsion. It seems, therefore, that those who abuse the release of dopamine (and other neurotransmitters), fall into depression. But why depression? It seems, to me, that depression offers the body a way of telling itself to slow down. To take less in. To stop and rest. When a person is depressed, his or her pupils are usually constricted. Why? Because the body is responding by "shutting down." The eyes do not want to take in visual data. The body does not want any stimuli. The body wants simply to rest. Basically, sometimes, we are "forced" into depression. Our body forces itself to be "slow," to be "depressed." The body does not want to find things entertaining. If something is entertaining, we stay awake all night seeking the pleasure. The pupils constrict—the eyes refuse to take anything in, they simply want the body to rest—to find everything and anything disinteresting, for the time being.

What will, then, in theory, happen to Lily and Mark? I think that most of us know the outcome. We know that somewhere along the line, things will not be so colorful. Lily will begin to look at Mark with not-so-dilated eyes (unless they are fighting!); Mark will begin to avoid Lily. But why does love end in such a way? I think that we have already discovered the answer. Humans must learn to live with a depressed state. Depression is as necessary to the human as is sleep. We must be happy that we are depressed! For happiness follows depression, like ice cream follows summer heat. Of course, everything can be taken to an extreme. I am not advocating depression. I am merely saying that we should recognize that we are humans, that we are not "made of metal." We need to rest, we need to sleep. We need to be depressed. We need to have the foot taken off of the gas pedal. Someone needs to refuel sometimes. We cannot just keep driving on the highway without ever stopping. Likewise, we cannot be happy without falling into a quasi-depression. By "quasi-depression" I mean something like "rest." I do not mean to say that we should all commit suicide the moment the dopamine stores run dry. I mean to say that we should all recognize that our body is just trying to tell us something. It is trying to say, "Slow down. Sleep a little here, skip dinner with your friends there. I just need to rest. Let me replenish the neurotransmitters, once that is done, go ahead, sail away."

So what is the solution? Can we ever avoid absolute depression? I think that we can. We can live life modestly and moderately. We can eat things in moderation (a little bit of this, a little bit of that) and we can live in moderation (we can laugh a little here, and cry a little there). Life is about striking a balance between the good and the bad. We cannot try to eliminate sleep. Likewise, we cannot eliminate the fact that our body will maintain homeostasis: our body will override our emotions and thoughts and make us submit to "upper management." We will slow down and have our energy restored to us. Thus, I suggest that people don't abuse their happiness (it will, inevitably, only be followed by conflict and depression). I suggest, along with the Greeks, that everything must be taken in moderation. Happiness included. We need to be happy, but be happy in such a way that our happiness becomes a cornerstone. A solid thread that is consistent and constant. We don't want to live a life of now-extremely-happy and now-extremely-depressed. We want to be humans that are as stable as possible. We want to be—to our other half—the shelter from the storm. A sturdy shelter. We cannot be like waves just taken with every drop in tide (James 1:6). It is nice to come home to a person who does not have extreme mood swings. I would rather come home to a wife that is constantly radiating a consistent happiness than come home to someone who is now *extremely* in love with me and then *extremely* disappointed with me. Let's start saving on neurotransmitters. Go green!

In conclusion, our bodies are constantly struggling to maintain a supply-and-demand society; we are constantly asking for either too much dopamine or not enough. We need to recognize our strengths and live within the boundaries of neurotransmitters. We need to be stable humans. To be stable, we must embrace our mortal existence and accept ourselves for who we are: mere human beings who are bound by the constraints of the flesh. Instead of making a big deal out of it, we must embrace our human condition. We need to simply try to be humans who are consistent. If we are happy and having lots of fun, we need to remember to eat and rest. We cannot be like the overly "happy" meth addict who forgets that food exists. Our attitude is constantly oscillating. That will never change. However, what we can change is how much we allow ourselves to "swing." We can swing like the pendulum, steadily, back and forth; or we can swing extremely to one side and then, in turn, extremely to the other. The oscillating factor is important to keep in mind in any and every relationship. Those who are depressed, should be more readily forgiven; they are, in the end, merely in "restoration mode." And those of us who are happy, should try to stimulate the proper use of dopamine. By being happy, we can infect others in a way that will stimulate dopamine production. For if you do not use it, you definitely lose it. Many things must be considered when trying to understand the supply-and-demand economy of our body. We shouldn't be too depressed, or force ourselves to "rest." For if we do, and step into the realm of extreme zeal, we can inhibit the production of dopamine. For if something is not "in demand," it goes "out-of-print" or "out-of-business." What we should do is strike a perfect balance. As to how one should go about doing that, only you can know.

CHAPTER THREE

The Only Thing Worth Living For Is Love

I was at a point in my life where logic had led to its grandest conclusions; a point where, like a mountain climber, I had already conquered the highest peaks. I had crossed fertile valleys and desert canyons; I had walked through thick and through thin, so to speak. The world lay before me as a complete puzzle; all of the puzzle pieces were in place. I had achieved everything that I had ever desired—a priceless education, a phenomenal talent and love for the liberal arts, and a vast knowledge of both the microscopic and seen world. I pursued knowledge like a man pursues the love of his life. I strived for it and sold my soul for its bittersweet embrace. I obtained knowledge and found it wanting. It's as if I have crossed the desert valley in search of water in order to find out that water was not what I needed, but food. Something of a dilemma was raised before me. I was tortured by the thought of being wrong. And wrong I was: knowledge brought death.

Rants on Love

Everything that I seen in this world amounted to nothing but futility, vanity, meaninglessness and hatred. The world was utterly cold and black. Bleak and hopeless. The things I loved gave me nothing in return. The reasons to love died within me. The girls I pursued left me in a worse state than when I began—the cruelty of women has been known to man since the beginning of mankind history. The vain cold shoulders I had suffered brought about nothing but only a reminder of how the world was unlike my own naivety. I would not get love in return for love. But neither would I get nothing in return: I would be served hatred. And the hate that the world offered would only be served more frequently and with increasing doses. I thought that I would be immune to hate; I thought that God would give me something to hold on to, some sort of shield, some armor that would protect me from anything that I didn't deserve. But I was wrong. Like so many before me, God remained silent. The blood of the martyr would only help quench the flames of love—and not the other way around. No longer did anything good serve its purpose. I confessed my own sins, but even then, anything good that one had had been turned into evil by the evil. Evil breeds evil, they say. Though I attempted my best at doing as much good unto others as I could; by no means was I perfect. However, by no means did I ever—with purpose—try to hurt someone or cause them any evil. Within my own power, I struggled to find some balanced good, something that pleased everyone. Nevertheless, I remained, as a saint, somewhat tainted. Forever a sinner, I.

But nothing kept me back from seeking utmost good. I strived to do good when served evil—I strived to imitate Christ in this mess of a cruel world. And all you end up with is a mass of self-pity and depression. You see the futility of life. Ask anyone on the street two questions: "Why do you live?" and "Why do you work?" Place the two questions side by side and make sure the person understands that they are intimately related. The person will respond by answering the second question—Why do you work?—by saying that he works to live. And when you ask him the first question—Why do you live?—he will respond either by a blank stare or by saying that he lives so that he may work. And then you would ask again, "Why do you work?" And he would say, "Because I need to feed my family. I need to pay for my food and their food." And then you would further ask him why he works to provide food. And he would respond by saying that he needs to live.

But, oh, to live! That is the real question! That is the paradox of eternity! Why do we live? Why do we go to work, in order so that we may live? Or do we live in order so that we may work? What is the purpose of human life?

I have asked myself this question roughly a hundred times a day for the past decade. And I will continue asking this question until my mind goes numb and my passion blends in with God's passion. Something about the setup makes it an impossible question to answer. Unless, of course, you lack enough resources to ponder the question.

I have only seen one thing in life: vanity. All is vanity. All is meaningless and futile. Depressing. Cold. Evil. Look at the evil done around you on a day-to-day basis. Even something as simple as writing a letter of friendship will get a negative response—or worse yet, no response at all. This evil that persists in humanity frightens me. It frightens me to the very centre of my core. My being is utterly famished. I lie exposed and exhausted. Simply frightened. No matter how much good you do, no matter what good you strive for, no matter what care you provide, no matter what kindness you handout, the world turns its back on you as if goodness meant nothing. And worse yet, it hurts most when it is done in the name of Christ.

Oh, pitiful creatures we are! We disgust even the dogs in our unjust actions. If only something or someone could awaken us. I rejoice at the joyful thought of being awakened from this coma.

I have not understood evil. I never attempted to understand it nor have I sought it out. It simply just got to me. It simply just became a part of me. Or should I say that it came very close to the centre of my heart—the very essence of my eternal soul. It hurt me to see that evil was close at hand. At the moments when I felt most a saint, the most evil I was served. At the times when I felt that I could love beyond imagination, I was given a cold shoulder.

At the time when I rejoiced at the hope that somehow and somewhere I would serve Christ, all my insides would be ripped open. This wretched turmoil has gotten the best of me. The years of harassment have left me passively cold. I no longer care for the world. No longer do I believe in hope. No longer do I strive to make this place better. I have become a creature of the past. I live one day at a time. I do not stray from the path of righteousness nor do I attempt to pay back evil with evil. My soul simply weeps. Truly I tell you, it never has stopped weeping. Something within me, this God-damned hope for the better. This life that screams for a breath of fresh air. Something in me longs for eternal "in Christ" mysticism. Something tells me that to be made perfect, one must become Christ incarnate. And the purity of the thought haunts me. For I am utterly imperfect.

I have lost my will. I do think that I have gained some sort of patience along the way, but the patience that I have gotten reveals nothing. I have learned to be temperate. Hardly do I ever get angry, and hardly do I ever express anything but tolerance. But it is the soul inside of me that is inextinguishable. Its silent cries can be heard only by those who choose to listen. Closely. Along the way, I have lost something. And this is what frightens me most. I cannot become as cold as the world. No matter what, I cannot become what the rumors say of me. I cannot become what atrocities others have done to me. I cannot become anything but myself. I must remain whatever it is that I am.

Rants on Love

This fragile man trapped in an eternal soul. This, truly, I am. I must be true to myself. I cannot hide any longer. I cannot just knowingly look away. Though sometimes I suffer in self-pity, I realize that somehow I must get back up again. I must do something. I cannot become what it is that they think I have become. And even then, those who think they know me, are merely strangers to me.

There is something that I have been holding back. It's something that I just couldn't get off my chest. I remember a time when I was a young and naïve boy. Oh, those days are like honey to my soul. In those times, I fell in love with a girl. I fell so madly in love with her that I was borderline insane. Something in me was alive. There was a fire that kept me going. And though some thought me strange, I was utterly hopeful. It really is hope that keeps mankind moving forward. I was hopeful of our love. I was so hopeful that I did not see the witch I had fallen for. It is precisely this that I have been holding back. Far too long now, I have blamed myself for everything. I would come up with various ways to prove my own incompetence or my own humanity. I would argue that everything was my fault. Sure, she had her faults, but I would strive to recognize my own. And this is where the problem lay. For I had been so self-absorbed in my own actions and thoughts, that I have failed to recognize who it was that I was in love with. For in reality it was never her.

She never existed.

This introspection eventually led to its obvious conclusion: absolute chaos. How could a person, who strived to love, end up with something absolutely contrary to his nature? How could a musician, by playing music, make anyone *un*musical? This is an eternal question that our most-wise Socrates had asked. And now I ask again. How is it that I could love someone, clothe them with all the love inside of me, and yet get hate in return? How is it that a letter of friendship can be given a cold shoulder? Have I not argued elsewhere that all human actions arise from one single action: God the Mover? And is not God good? Then why do we have evil? And now I have received a sort of contradictory answer: because love does not always breed love, it simply opens doorways to more love, but those doorways to enter are left entirely up to the one who is receiving the love to enter. And so it is with evil, evil does not always breed evil—it simply opens up doorways to more evil, but those doorways to enter are left entirely up to the one who is receiving the evil to enter. This clearly explains how Christ, though in all of His sufferings, could have showered all humanity with His eternal love. For Christ did not return evil for evil, but love for evil. He *chose* love. I chose everything. I chose whether I will despise the girls that have hurt me, or whether I, like Christ, will love them and serve them with a humility that is second to none. That is my own choice.

This choice, though, was a hard choice to make. For I had reached the peaks of knowledge. And that ruined the moment. The moment when I was supposed to peer over the ridge and see the sunset, I was busy contemplating the meaninglessness of knowledge. I had journeyed so far to discover that what I was searching for served, to an extent, no true purpose. I contemplated all of the evil done to me and all of the self-pity that I had experienced. I had contemplated, further, any harm that I have done unto others. Whether intentional or not, I had to repent. And repent I did. Or at least I tried. But repentance was not to come easy. For in my love for wisdom, I had lost something. I had lost eternity. I had traded in my eternal soul for a scrap of ever-rusting knowledge. I had lost the good fight, or so I thought. Nonetheless, something in me died. I was tired of playing useless and childish games. Whether it was romance or theology, I was tired of learning from guess-and-check. Those around me, lusted after games that served no meaning. For example, even in inter-sex relations, I have come to observe how society has turned everything into a sort of game: don't do this, do that; if she doesn't respond in 2 days, buy this on the third day; if he tells you *this* on the second week, it means *that*, etc. I was tired of the futility of the quest. I was tired of pursuing girls who had no idea of what it meant to serve God and to serve humanity. Girls who had no idea what it felt like to be madly and passionately in love. Girls that could not, and *would not*, comprehend passion. This patient and temperate so-called love and "passion" was a thorn in my side—this societal dream was as absurd as hot ice. It was insane.

As regards theology, I was tired of knowledge. It served no true purpose. I began to agree with Kierkegaard; namely, knowledge is not entirely what it claims to be. In fact, knowledge was to be taken by faith. Faith was greater than knowledge. One must take leaps of faith in order to please both God and man.

But what was knowledge? Knowledge is something that one "knows." It is something that exists only inside the human mind. Animals do have knowledge, but that means nothing in this discussion. Since knowledge is directly relational to the existence of a mind, it is only fair to ask if "knowledge" really exists. And it appears that it, in reality, does not. For if one were to take away the human mind, and destroy all life on earth, where would "knowledge" be? Nowhere. It would cease to exist.

So the question that bothered me was this: if I was seeking knowledge in order to find God (eternal), how could something as knowledge (non-eternal/temporal) know anything about God (the eternal)? If God was eternal, and knowledge was not, why did knowledge matter? (For it should be obvious that in heaven, at least in theory, knowledge ceases to exist. For it is not eternal.) In the eternal heavens, when the fleshly body ceases to exist, knowledge dies. And with knowledge dies all of man's horrors and tragedies of life.

In my desperate prayers offered to God, He only told me one thing. When I was at my wits end and seeking an answer, a relief, I best call it, from God, I got a response that pleased me. At the time when I felt that annihilation of my soul was the only meaningful thing left, God told me something I will never forget. And, at that time, those words were so smooth and warm. They were, at least to me, intensively meaningful and beautiful.

He told me, "Knowledge is not eternal."

And that was it. Everything seemed to make sense. If knowledge is not eternal, then knowledge would not haunt me in heaven. It would not haunt me in the hereafter. For me that was something. I was frightened at the mere thought of knowing the past evil done in God's name and in man's name. I was frightened that knowledge would stunt our ability to experience love. For only in true knowledge does one realize that knowledge is evil. What is knowledge? It is surely a thing of the past. Knowledge is knowing something about something. It is knowing how one thing relates to another. Knowledge is, predominantly, a thing of the certain past: for only in retrospect can knowledge be obtained and only then can it have meaning. But why have knowledge? For example, I know that, for a fact, a girl I like gave me a cold shoulder. My "knowledge" of the event would only breed contempt and evil. How does the "knowledge" help one live a good life? It doesn't. This is why love keeps no track of wrongs. On the other hand, one may refute me by saying that "knowledge" is good because it helps you recall good and romantic memories. But that is simply not true. One only "recalls" and "remembers" good memories when one is not making any better ones! It is ironic! Had the person been involved in a romantic relationship at the moment, he would never have wasted time contemplating something of the past. Why would you waste time daydreaming about passionate love when passionate love surrounds you at the very moment? This clearly demonstrates that "knowledge" is entirely evil. For in remembering evil actions, it serves as a reservoir for vengeance, evil, and retribution; for in remembering good, and recalling the romantic past, knowledge presupposes that one is not experiencing the romantic in one's own real time. Thus, knowledge truly serves no purpose.

Imagine a day like this, with no knowledge: you would wake up in the morning, full of God's love, and you would go out and love the world equally. You would love your wife, you would love your family, and you would love your neighbor. You would not know anything of the good things or the bad things anyone had done. In fact, most of the time "knowledge" keeps track of the good things done in order so that it could keep in check how much good one returns! (Only multiplying evil in return.) Imagine this world for a minute. A world without knowledge. A world where everyone loves, for there is nothing else to do. If one were to choose to do evil, one could, in such a world. However, the evil done would be forgotten the moment it would be contemplated. But why would someone, in such a world, choose evil? Most of the time, people choose evil in order to pay someone back. Or they choose evil because of some misconception about someone or something. In a world without knowledge, one could not do evil to Mr. Smith who… *who did what? Mr. Smith did nothing to you, remember? Oh, I forgot, you cannot remember anything.* Imagine for a second. John wants to murder James. John goes out at night to murder James, but he forgets the reasons for his having desired the death of James. What would happen? Would evil or murder still be done? No! How could a person kill someone who did nothing (literally)? In a world without this form of knowledge, things would be grand.

After I had experienced my "dark night of the soul," I decided that love was still worth it. Someday and somehow, everything would turn out okay. I would give love and get love in return. I would do good and not worry about evil. I long for such a world. It is, by all means, a heaven. And all one has to do to create it is choose love. Love is free. It is a doorway that I have pushed open for you. Love's Door calls out to you and beckons you, "Come to me all who are weary. Enter in. For I will bring you eternal peace." Go on.

Go ahead, do enter in. It is free. There are no costs involved. Love is a choice. It has always been and it will always be. It is eternal. Love is that free hug, love is that passionate kiss. Love asks nothing. All it asks is to be passed on. Pass love on.

CHAPTER FOUR

The Vainness of Marital Love: Why Romantic Love Surpasses Marital Love in Passion

Recently, a radical idea has been proposed to me: the futility of marital love. Søren Kierkegaard, a 19th century Christian philosopher, proposed a relatively simple analogy that demonstrated the futility of marital love. He supposed that if a poem were written about romantic love it would focus on the moments leading up until the consummation of absolute passion; namely, the kiss, the embrace, or maybe the sex. He supposed that if a man spent fifteen years wooing a girl, at the end of the fifteen years, he would get something for all of the effort. For example, after waiting patiently for a girl for fifteen years, the poet would describe all of the lonesome nights and all of the tortuous delayed moments of gratification. Eventually, the poet would describe the moment that absolute passionate love was consummated as *the moment*. This moment I call "the *kairos*" (from the Greek word ΚΑΙΡΟΣ, which means "opportune moment [when something special happens]"). In the *kairos*, the couple that has delayed gratification until a certain point, explodes with absolute infatuated passion. This special moment (*kairos*) could have happened on the infamous wedding night or even at the time of the first kiss. In recent times some form of *kairos* has been occurring outside the bounds of marriage, but this lustful love stands infinitely like an infidel in comparison to the true *kairos*. Therefore, all modern ideas of passionate love must be disregarded as inferior infidels that have nothing to do with absolute passion—for the modern forms of love know nothing of modesty, self-control and delayed gratification. Now, in the true *kairos*, the moments leading up until the *kairos* itself are moments filled with restraint and self-control—these moments could be compared to *coitus interruptus*; just before the moment ends in fruition, the moment is delayed. Pre-*Kairotic* moments are similar in this regard: they form isolated moments of delayed gratification that lead to *the* moment of all time; namely, the *kairos*.

Kierkegaard, in bringing the romantic poem as an example of how romantic love is superior to marital love, demonstrated that after the fifteen years of delayed gratification, the enchanted and now impatient man gets *something* after the infinite wait; he gets either that special kiss or the hand in marriage. Nonetheless, *something* is gotten from the nights of excruciating torture and nights of hopeless romance. That something is precisely what I have labeled the *kairos*. This moment, this passion, this consummation of infinite, infatuated, passionate love explodes in a single moment of beloved expression. It is absolutely this moment alone that I am talking about when speaking about the *kairos*.

Now, in contrast to this *kairotic* and supreme form of love, Kierkegaard mentioned marital love and how such love stood in absolute contrast to romantic, *kairotic* love. (Though the terms *kairotic* are of my own invention—I have built upon what Kierkegaard has mentioned in certain passing.) The question now that should be asked is this: What does marital love—in contrast with romantic love—have to offer? What is it that is obtained from this union of two people? Is anything gotten out of marital love? Does marital love serve a purpose? Is there anything that delays gratification in marital love? Are there pre-*kairotic* moments that lead to the absolute and most wonderful *kairos*? The answer stands as a solemn and horribly resounding "No!" It is the most awful sound. That sound of "No." What does the man in the marital poem—in contrast to the romantic poem—gain? Does his love consummate in something grander and more glorious? It appears not. The man who is married gets nothing from marriage; he does not experience absolute *kairos* nor does he obtain the girl's hand in marriage (for that had already been accomplished), neither does he lust after that kiss (for that is offered upon request). Where, then, is the passion that has been so long talked about that supposedly exists in marriage? Where is it to be found? Kierkegaard rightly asserted that romantic love must be distinguished from marital love.

Moreover, what is gained when one marries? One has *everything to lose in marriage.* The love of the man's life may die. She may divorce him. Maybe she will cheat on him. Maybe their kids would end up being handicaps. Maybe they will have no kids. Maybe someone will die in an accident. These are the thoughts that haunt the married man. These are the thoughts that are given in return for marital love. How grand, then, and inferior, is marital love! It pales in contrast to romantic love! It appears to be the most wicked thing created since sin. A love that only demands. A love that only takes and extinguishes all flames of a dying romance. This, then, is what marital love is.

But now, look at romantic love. A love that has nothing but absolute commitment. For it is deceptive to think that marital love has the greatest form of commitment; nay, romantic love requires the greater of the two commitments. Look at romantic love, for example. In romantic love, one must wait and delay gratification for, say, a couple years on end. The story of Jacob and Rachel clearly demonstrates the perfect example of this form of commitment. Would it be wise to say that Jacob was *not* committed to Rachel? No! That would be insanity. It was precisely Jacob's non-marital love that gave prowess to commitment. Jacob was a man that had the greatest of commitments; in fact, it would be wrong to say that he remained as committed after he got married. Now that would be deceptive. On the other hand, in marital love, the only commitments brought forth are dry, mundane things like taking care of children, paying rent, and providing food. How are these greater commitments than that which romantic love requires? I think that an answer is not required; for it is self-evident. Thus, I say that romantic love is not only most passionate, it is also the most committed. Now, I will also point out that marital love also has its commitments, but that must not be confused with consummated gratification—for in marital love one already gets what one wanted. If one wanted children, one got children; if one wanted a wife, one got a wife. According to logic, one would not say that if one obtained a wife, one obtained an unfair commitment. The rules of nature tell us that one cannot blame chance or anything else when one gets what one wanted. Therefore, marital love, with all of its so-called unbearable commitments, is not a commitment *per se* that must be complained about (for one only got what one asked for); such is the unbearable excuse that an *uncommitted* person offers. It appears, therefore, that marital love has not the assumed greater of commitments. In fact, as has been shown, marital love only gets what it has asked for—nay, even demanded!—thus, it is irrational to call marital love a commitment when one already gets, and has, what one so wanted.

To further demonstrate my point, I will bring another reason in defense of romantic love. Romantic love is the greater of commitments because it hinges on absolute faith. What I mean is this: all of the sleepless nights and all of the delayed moments of gratification could be taken away at will. If the girl decides that the relationship must be declared over, then so it is. If the man decides the same, so it is also. In romantic love, there is a certain point that appears out of the murky waters of love that brings along with it uncertainty; for it is not certain that the man would end up with the girl he so passionately desires. In romantic love, there is a risk involved that is superior to all other risks. Therefore, romantic love carries with it a sort of supernatural faith and an amazing load of adrenalin. This is what makes romantic love so beautiful.

To be sure, romantic love is consummated in a single moment we have called the *kairos*. However, it is certain that marital love can also have its kairotic moments. What I mean is this: if a married couple so wills, it can have nights of abstinence in preparation for the *kairos*. There are, I am sure, a multitude of ways to delay gratification even within the strict bounds of marriage. Thus, as the argument now stands, it appears that both romantic love and marital love are similar; namely, the loves overlap. You could be involved in a marriage that contains *kairotic* moments and infatuated passion. But such moments must be built and created (and waited for patiently).

In spite of the differences and similarities, I want to point out an even greater form of love: the recalled moment. In order to experience the recalled moment, one must recall romantic moments, but only in one's memory. Some, like Kierkegaard, have thought that such moments must be recalled only when the real (reality) does not really exist. What I mean is this: in order for one to experience a recalled moment, one must be disconnected from reality. One must break the relationship with a girl, for example, when it is at its peak; just before the fruition of the *kairos*—this is what Kierkegaard did after being engaged for one year to Regine Olsen. He broke the engagement and forever recalled and relived the pre-*kairotic* moment. After the break, one must cease to relive anything realistically; everything must be only recalled in memory. Such a form of love is eternal, passionate, satisfying, and unchangeable; for nothing can change it. Such a love exists in the eternal mind and does not associate with the likes of the temporal and the fleshly. This love is, to be sure, very hard to achieve. Relatively few people could live up to its standards.

But even here, Kierkegaard was, I think, somewhat misled. For the recalled moment could be experienced by someone who is married. One must simply learn to forget the evil. One must recall the romantic moments and forget those moments that lacked the passion of romance. This, I believe, can be done. It is no wonder that Albert Schweitzer said that, "Happiness is nothing more than good health and a bad memory." Thus, I believe that marital love does not only qualify to contain the "recalled moment," but it also qualifies to be called romantic love. For romantic love is proportional to one's ability to restrain oneself. This is the key to any form of infatuated passion.

Now that I have briefly called to mind a few different forms or variations of love, I think it necessary to reflect on one's own ability to maintain such a love. I, personally, think that I have come to a point in my life that demands attention; namely, it is becoming constantly more apparent that I am unsuitable to be a husband. Just as Kierkegaard argued that any man was preferable as a husband than him, so do I think that any man is preferable to be a husband than me. My passion may be superior than most men's but that is because I am skilled at delaying gratification and skilled at restraining myself and my passions. No wife wants a philosopher for a husband. That has been declared from of old and is most definitely a true saying. An introspective person is not competent for marriage nor is he suitable to be a marital lover. Though some may find passion, as that of Kierkegaard's, as admirable, however, one cannot miss the fact that it is such precisely because of no gratification whatsoever. It is this that sets him apart from the majority of philosophers at large. Passion is the end result of self-control and restraint. Everything in moderation is what the Greeks taught. Passion, when bridled, breeds passion. May my own passion die with me. And may God help me.

CHAPTER FIVE

Canned Dating and Other Disposable Inter-Sex Relationships

I have observed a few things in my short stay here on Planet Earth. Now, these "things" are, by all means, biased—if by "biased" you mean that I have purposefully selected the type of people I hung out with and the sort of information I have allowed myself to be exposed to. In that sense, yes, I am very biased; I have lived my life (like every other human being) by enjoying friendships with people that I was compatible with. The things I observed can be very controversial and not everyone may agree. In this paper, I care not for what is politically-correct or for what is the dominant view. Here, I only speak as a person who speaks not from knowledge of the world at large, but from absolute personal experience. Which means a few things: (1) The information will be very biased; (2) The information will contain things that only I have observed (and nobody else); and (3) The information may not be suitable for all audiences. When a person claims to make statements or write papers only from absolute personal experience, you are bound to be politically-incorrect and socially awkward. What do I mean by "absolute personal experience"?

Personal experience, apart from the general holistic worldview that is propagated by the masses, is different because it ignores the "general" idea about any given fact or thing. For example, I recently met a young man who sounded like a racist. At first, I thought he was. However, he wasn't. He told me his life experience growing up in the ghetto and how the black kids there would gang beat him sometimes. Obviously, such a person has, to an extent, a "right" to be upset with the way the "other race" had treated him. Similarly, the Jews to this day may be somewhat wary of the Germans, and for good reason. On a sociological level, we all know that not all black people beat white kids who live in the ghetto, and we all know that not all Germans throw Jews into campfires while roasting marshmallows. However, in spite of the general view (the dominant view), there exists a *personal view*. It is personal and expresses what had been experienced by that particular person alone, without bothering to factor in what had been experienced by others in this world. In this paper, I will be peddling a personal view. It is a view that I *personally* have lived through or have experienced in my *own* life. I want to deal with the issue of what I have come to call "canned dating" or "disposable relationships." I will not take into account what researchers such as John Gottman have found or what David Schnarch had discovered. I am here to talk about relationships between men and women as *I* have seen them through my very *own* eyes. I will ignore all the books I have read. And I will ignore what I think may be the actual answer to a particular question. The view that modern dating is both "canned" and "disposable" is most likely not new; I am certain that others have written books on the view (though they must have called it something else). Such books will not be taken into consideration here. I am here to burst some bubbles and long-cherished views. (And I am adamant about being a heretic and *not* an orthodox thinker.)

Canned dating is what most people are experiencing today. Canned dating is what people do because they have not yet learned how to have meaningful inter-sex relations. For centuries now, men have been viewed as *predators* and women have been viewed as *prey*. (Sadly, I will not be refuting that view here—though I will try to convince others to redefine it and overhaul it.) Men have predominantly been the observers and women have been the ones being observed. Because men have dominated the field of observation for centuries (before women were allowed to write books and get educated), men have, inevitably, gained profound knowledge regarding the female mind. We have dissected it and now have fully understood the intricate and most intimate details regarding any woman's emotions/actions (women usually have more emotions than men will be ever capable of producing). In all of our studies, we have learned a few vital things: no one knows more about women than men—and men know nothing. In spite of the difficulties, men have realized that there is really *nothing* to know. We have been looking for gold in a cat's litter box; we have been looking for a quality product at Wal-Mart. And our quest was bound to be fruitless. You cannot expect to find water in the desert, just like you cannot expect to find *something* where there really is *nothing*. Men have come to realize, since June 17th, 2011, that there is nothing to look for. One needs not knowledge to know how to operate a woman. They are very simple creatures—in comparison to a modern TV set. All one needs is access to a remote. And that remote has been *us* all along! Men have long held the remote control in their very hands! No, in fact, they, themselves, have been the remote! If a woman is a TV set, a man is the remote control. Ever since man has discovered this (and it has not yet been a day), we have realized that the remote has been missing the batteries all along. And that almost brought us to tears. Nonetheless, men, we have an answer—err, I have an answer. Or so I think.

Most modern relationships revolve around a few faulty notions: (1) Men must be the predators; (2) Women must be the prey. Both ideas are inherently wrong in themselves. And women have been the problem. (At least, I think, they should have realized [it's about flippin' time] that being the *prey* is *not* a good thing!) Nevertheless, women failed to change. Women failed to recognize the consequences of being the prey. The consequences were like a bad scene from the *Discovery Channel*—where the lion eats the gazelle—with all of the blood and guts. Not a good thing. Thus, I think it is about time that men have stepped up to the plate and have offered a solution. A long needed solution. And I'm offering my two cents worth. Right now. Free of charge. (Donations will be accepted. Please mail checks that are greater than six digits to 567 East Sharp Avenue…)

First of all, back to what I originally said, women are not prey. So long as they continue to act like prey, they will end up in disposable relationships and end up being sold at the supermarket in the Canned Dating Goods section. If that's what you females want, well, don't listen to my advice and continue living as you were: continue being the prey. I, on the other hand, want to help save the female species from dying out. (Superman has got nothing on me!) Therefore, I am adamant about pushing forth this new view unto the scene. However, even with the new view, there will be eternal repercussions felt until the day Jesus Christ returns. (*Marana tha* [Aramaic for "Our Lord, Come!"]) In spite of the inevitable (and trifle) difficulties, I propose this new model for relationships, on the grounds that it will work better than canned dating has worked for Grandma Jane and Grandpa Max.

Women need to redefine the idea of prey. They must start with first overhauling the notion of what it means to be *simple prey* and *sexy prey* (there is a world of difference). *Simple prey* are things that are at the bottom of the food chain and run away when something larger than an ant starts chasing it (most modern women fall into this category). *Sexy prey* are women who know their worth, but who refuse to be prey (in the literal animal kingdom kind of sense). You should have noticed by now that women, whether they like it or not, still remain "prey" even with this new model on relationships. Sorry ladies, I can't find a better word to use. Plus, ladies, you loved to be wooed. And wooing presupposes your status as social prey. Now, as bad as it may sound at first, this is an excellent idea that God would have mentioned in the Bible had I been around to write that section. Since God failed to talk about sexy prey, I think it is my God-given job to do that. So, please listen carefully. (I think God winked at me.)

I would like to first demonstrate the modern methods used in canned dating relationships. First, the man, being the predator, looks at a woman, the prey, and falls instantly "in love." (Of course, this is nothing but a lack of oxygen content in the brain stem related to the effects of decreased blood perfusion in the brain, secondary to an enormous erection.) The man "chases" the woman (the simple prey) while she runs around like a mouse being chased by a fox. And run she does. (In all of evolutionary history, the only thing women have perfected is their ability to run from men!) The man (being the determined predator, as his father, the infamous orangutan, has taught him so well) continues to chase the woman. He chases. And he chases. And he chases. Chases. Chases.

And then the chase. Ends. Boom.

All of a sudden, the horrific fox (the man) becomes a Prince Charming in the eyes of the infatuated girl (the mouse in the story). Yes, just like some ancient had once said, the frog turned into the prince.

The moment the male stops chasing the girl, the girl starts sucking up to the male. And then the fox enters a canned dating relationship with the mouse and life continues. Not. The male ends up dating a disposable mouse and eventually ends up disinterested in the mouse's abilities to satisfy him. So the relationship is disposed of and the mouse looks for someone else to woo to chase her. This is the state most modern relationships are in.

Now, what is St. Moses proposing? First, I am proposing a radical parting with this view. I propose (where the heck is the 10-carat diamond ring?!) that we redefine what it means for women to be prey. Women must stop being what I have labeled "simple prey." They need to grow up and start acting like mature human beings. Stop being the mouse in the freakin' story! It's as simple as that! Begin by acting like *sexy prey*. What do I mean by this? Women need to know their worth. They don't need to arrogantly rub it in (for that will end in an extreme reaction from the male species, which will end in the extermination of the *weaker* female sex). Women need to behave themselves and carry themselves as equals, both in the sight of men and in the sight of God. St. Paul would whole-heartedly agree with me (though not the author of 1 Timothy).

To be *sexy prey*, women need to stop being chased. You are only as good as the chase, then. If you want more than a stupid relationship that is more focused on the act of the chase than it is focused on meaningful discussion, then you need to part with the old and outdated view: *simple prey*. I ask all women to part with this model and begin living their lives as equals. Not prey. So long as the female body continues to sell itself for sexual purposes, it will suffer the consequences of orthodox inequality. So long as the female mind continues to "run" from the male, so long will women bear the consequences of inequality. Women must rise to what I call an *equal sexy prey status*. The longer a woman "runs" from a male, the more of a prey she becomes. Face it. Stop running! Start *talking*! If you don't want a male chasing you, open up. Reveal your dirty secrets and we'll end our pursuit. Stop running. If you continue to run, you automatically fall into the simple prey category. Remember this: Prey Run, Predators Chase. If you continue to run from men, and continue using methods such as "cold shoulder" or "ignoring bliss," you will be unequal, both in the sight of God and man (and the animal kingdom).

Rants on Love

Now, my attention is turned to the male species. Men need to grow some balls and take a hold of their inner inhibitions. They need to practice self-control. No more *PlayBoy* or one-night stands for you. Men who feed on prey are just as horrible as the women who sell themselves short. Either men grow up, shed their birth control pills, and start acting like equals, or they will continue living with women who are *simple prey* and nothing more. And men will continue the cycle of canned dating. However, if men shed this old and outdated mode of thinking, we can rise to a status consisting of respect, honesty and integrity.

There is no need to continue this vicious cycle of disposable relationships. Animals exchange their mates like they change their socks (had they had the brains to make any). However, unless you want to believe a thinker like Charles Darwin, start acting not like a mere animal, but as a human being, who carries the very breath of God. And that includes women, men.

So, in conclusion, if women allowed dialogue, we would not have problems. It's about time people realized that men "chase" women in order to discover their character, and women run from men thinking that men "want" them (when, in fact, a man is only seeking to find out if you truly are worth the pursuit). So, let's cut the crap, and start acting like grownups. If women continue running from men when engaging in inter-sex relations, they will continue to be viewed as prey (for only the weak prey runs). If, on the other hand, women take men on in debate and dialogue, and engage in meaningful discussion early on in the dating game, a purposeful relationship will soon follow. The game of life is not a game, nor is it based on the way wild animals do things; namely, chase and run. It's time for women to view themselves as more than *simple prey*. And they can begin now. Not every guy talking to you or hitting on you is really "interested" in you (in the strict literal sense of the word). He is merely discovering your character as a normal human being. Give him a chance. He'll figure you out and eventually willingly leave you alone. If you start "running," you are merely stooping down to the status of humble (and detestable) simple prey.

Make a change. Shed your animal kingdom/food chain mentality and we will all be alright. Take us on in dialogue and we'll surprise you with our wit and humor. God bless all of those who will take a stand and begin living life as equals and not as mere animals. (By the way, sorry for being politically-incorrect. Just once.)

CHAPTER SIX

How To Know People: An Introduction to Chaos Social Theory, As Presented by a Hardcore Existentialist

All of life is chaos. One large act of chaos. We are born into a war that rages on endlessly and meaninglessly. We look for meaning at the mess that we are born into; we seek to find patterns and attempt to make sense of all that comes our way. Our very existence is chaotic. All humans must accept this. I would like to provide at least one simple example from everyday life. This will help establish what I am setting out to prove.

Once upon a time there was a boy. He was 24 years old and he was a Christian. He was born in France and spoke French. He ended up coming to America and met a girl who was American. They both fell in love. She was a militant atheist.

Now there are a few things with this scenario that must be examined critically. We must first step back and look at the data as nonchalantly and unbiased as possible.

The boy is Christian and the girl is an atheist. These terms have meaning because society gave them meaning; it imparted meaning upon them. The girl, who was raised in America, who labeled herself a militant atheist, would probably believe certain things which society deemed she, being a "militant atheist," should believe. But the boy, who grew up in a different country, would not be aware of all of the terminological baggage; in other words, he would be, right off the bat, misunderstanding her and creating an impression of her which does not exist. Because his creation of her is not what actually corresponds to reality, this means that he is creating an *illusion* of the girl. Because she is an *illusion*, this creates chaos. Hence my terminology.

From the moment that the girl met the boy, there was chaos. In the beginning there was chaos and nothing but chaos. What do I mean by that? Well, the boy met a girl who stood before him as an object. An object labeled "atheist." This object he could only respond to via the senses. He would examine her height, her eye color, her hair color, etc. He would catch a scent of her and probably taste her lips at some point. He would talk with her and hear her speak words to him. These words would then be imparted to his brain where he would dissect the content and try to make sense of the data.

What is going on here?

What is going on is that this boy who met this girl is creating an *illusion* of her. I call this an illusion because outside of reality, he would never (and will never) truly "know" her in any meaningful sense (from an empirical perspective). All that he will know—in this life—is that illusion of her that he created, which exists only in his mind (and may, *or may not*, correspond to the historical figure [i.e., the girl]). This girl which this boy met exists—for him. But she exists in his mind. He communicates thoughts with her, he listens to her sing, he kisses her on the lips before bedtime, etc., but she is never his. She never is *known* by him.

She is a stranger.

Now, this girl could love this boy very much. She could reinforce some of his ideas about her. She could verify and validate her feelings and he would then, I assume, toss her words into his cerebrum and make sense of the data (again). What is going on here? What is going on here is reinforcement of illusionary factors. First, the boy falls in love with a girl. Then he creates an image or illusion of her in his mind. This image is then reinforced or deconstructed by the girl.

For example, let us suppose that the boy thought the girl was patient. However, upon marriage, the boy discovers that she is not patient. A number of things could happen. The boy could tell the girl what he thinks and she could either *validate* his ideas or *deconstruct* them. (Depending on which she chooses, he will create an illusion of her that resembles the historical figure either accurately or less accurately.) This process could be labeled "creation" or "formation." It is here that people create illusions of one another. They create illusions that may or may not actually exist.

But what do we mean by "existence" and "historical figure"? I take this to mean the actual human being. By "actual human being" I mean the human being that is the sum of all activities. Thus, for example, if a person is a pacifist in most situations—and only murders on occasion—then such a person is essentially a "pacifist." Of course, one could debate this and stress the fluidity of human nature here (which I completely agree with) but, for the sake of categorization and (my very own) illusion formation, I will pretend that humans are somewhat stable and change minimally.

What then does this boy "know" about the girl? Well, in my opinion, very little. It will take years of living with a person before you ever "know" the person. Before you ever come even close to creating an illusion that matches the historical figure in any significant way. This is why all of life is chaos.

If marriage creates *accurate illusion formation*, then non-marriage relationships are pretty much all illusions that should be critically doubted. Of course, family members are probably safe at creating an accurate assessment of a given historical figure.

This implies much for the world. This brief essay shows that it is impossible to really "know" people. The only people we "know" are people whom we have been with for years. And even then we may not know the person. Especially if any sort of "change" in personality is involved (a paradigm shift). A paradigm shift could be a religious conversion experience or something along those lines.

What do we, as people, do once we have this basic knowledge? I say that we accept chaos. We should accept this and move on. We should realize that our relationships with other humans are very fragile—fragile indeed! Our loved ones must be cherished and we must move past our own inaccurate illusion formations. We must advance towards realizing what is real—what is reality. We crave reality. (Which is why virtual relationships almost never satisfy.) We crave to be known and we crave to know. I once wrote a song that had lyrics that went like this: "I don't have to, if I don't want to; I just want to hold you close, to know you and to be known." I am arguing for a chaotic existence. However, I am also arguing that this knowledge presented in this paper forces us to look at life more critically and forces us to attempt to create meaningful relationships with people. We must strive to live an *authentic* life. A life in which we are known by people and known to ourselves; a life in which we act as we are and are known for those actions accurately.

CHAPTER SEVEN

A Philosophical Look at 'Unconditional Love': The Irrationality of Such a Love

Many lovers have said something along the lines of, "I love you, baby, unconditionally. No matter *what* happens, I will *always* love you." Others would say something similar, except maybe in different words, echoing the belief that humans are capable of what has philosophically been termed "unconditional love." Though many sincere lovers have repeated this, I have decided to once-and-for-all refute such insane statements. I will demonstrate here the irrationality of such an "unconditional" love and the meaninglessness of it. On the other hand, I will argue that such a love does exist, except in a form *unbeknownst* to humans before the writing of this exposition on love. This love—this truly unconditional love—can only exist in the realm of the invisible, abstract, and divine. This sort of love is not *merely* divine—it *is* God.

First, we must define the terms that will be used throughout this exposition on love. By "unconditional love," one must inevitably mean a love that exists apart from predetermined conditions—or, in other words, a love that exists *in spite* of certain conditions. I think that, in the real world, the second definition is more realistic, practical and genuine. (That is, only if you trust my judgment.) In the real world, i.e., the world that we now live in, "unconditional love" is a love that exists in spite of certain conditions. The phrase "in spite of" is purposefully used to connote a negative atmosphere surrounding such a love. The reason for such pessimistic negativism is as follows:

(1) I would not need to emphasize, when I love a girl, that I would love her unconditionally—by stating things thus, I *presuppose* the fact that horrible things are bound to happen, and I will, *in spite* of these terrible conditions, still love her.

(2) By emphasizing my love using such phrases as "unconditional" and "no matter what," I am clearly alluding to the fact that evil things will happen and that I will ignore them—however, using such words creates the false illusion of such a thing as unconditional love, which doesn't, in the sense that

moderns take it, even exist. Therefore, the words that I use carry forth no meaning and end up being derided.

Since I have demonstrated that "unconditional love" presupposes a negative atmosphere, I want to, briefly, ask the question that no one really asks: Why is such negative love elevated to such an exalted status? If by "unconditional love" you envision a world of evil, pain and suffering, why would you want to *impose* such a love and use it in a romantic relationship? Wouldn't it be *more* romantic *not* to state such things as "no matter what"? However, because humanity continues to be ignorant as to what love really is, we will continue to have such ridiculous talk—albeit, coming from teenagers!—that love is unconditional (and *that* is *so* romantic!). What frightens me most, however, is the fact that people toss around words so freely, so loosely, so as to stimulate the death of their meaning. People toss around phrases such as "unconditional love" without ever *thinking* about what such a phrase entails. It isn't shocking, since our society isn't keen on producing great philosophers, we prefer to have dull theologians. People must, first, understand the terminology and the meaning of the words they use. Unconditional love presupposes a detachment from "conditions." But what are conditions?

A condition is a "state," a "clause," a "circumstance" or a "form." It is the *fine print*. In other words, it is some sort of *restraint*. It is the seatbelt that keeps the body from flying out of the vehicle in an accident. It is something almost *palpable*. For example, a condition could be hair color, or, more generally, beauty. Someone may state that in order for him to like a certain girl, she *must* be beautiful. Of course, we all have our own definition of beauty—which is found in the eyes of the beholder—nonetheless, a prerequisite such as "beauty" is, by definition, a condition. If that *condition* is not met, then the alleged love ceases to exist (from a philosophical perspective, I would argue that it never existed!). To put it a different way, a condition could be a characteristic. For example, a woman could love a man in his state of soberness; however, the moment he became intoxicated, her love would cease to exist—or, more appropriately, it would be put on hold. The presupposition is that love—her love—must be maintained in a "sober environment." The moment the man drinks is the moment the conditions—the fine print—are not being met. This is the moment that terminates the contract that exists between the couple—and it *is* a contract—and the love recedes into the shadows in hopes of a better day. A conditional love is a *contractual love*. It involves two parties who agree to love one another upon the implementation of the required conditions. It is a love that requires two people to agree to love one another because of certain requirements which are—at the moment!—being met. This is conditional love at its core. And it isn't as ugly as we think it is—in fact, it's very beautiful. You know why? Because we are all doing it.

Those of you who still believe in the myth of unconditional love should congratulate yourselves for being hypocrites. (I do feel sorry for you, such disillusioned beings!) It is a matter of fact that you (and me—in fact, all of us) are *not* engaging in *any* form of true unconditional love *per se*. It is impossible to love unconditionally. Impossible. Period. In fact, I am divinely inspired when saying this. My words are infallible. It is impossible for a human being living on planet earth to love another human being unconditionally. Impossible.

What human beings actually engage in is a form of conditionally-unconditional love. It sounds like paradox but—let me assure you—it isn't. It's actually relatively simple. Humans love one another with certain conditions. For example, generally speaking, we like to stick to our own kind. Asians marry Asians, Russians marry Russians, Americans marry Americans, etc. We like people who are like us. We stay within our own circles. There are a few odd balls here and there, but they are of no special significance—they merely want attention. The general masses go according to the rules—divine laws?—of nature: set conditions, then love. The conditions being set here are simple: marry someone of your own race or kind. And believe me, that is a condition. One must ask here if such a thing as that is actually bad. The sociological answer is an emphatic no. What is wrong with marrying someone who shares a similar cultural background? If I had no conditions, and loved "unconditionally," I would walk up to some Eskimo, fall in love, get married and *no speako thee langveege*. That would suck. Imagine our conversation after our first night of marriage:

Moses to Eskimo Wife Who Speaks Unidentifiable Language: "Hey, love, that was wonderful!"

Eskimo Wife: "Q'who al Shmath efth la Maryt I'shesh Ma-Jaba le ma heem!"

Moses: "Wow, you are so right, I do love Olive Garden!"

I think such "unconditional love" would not last long after the initial interest in unknown sex fades. What would last, however, is the *stupid* notion that love is "unconditional"!

One must seriously consider whether love is unconditional or not. Sociologically speaking, humans must—generally—remain within their own sphere of understanding. In theory, anyone could marry someone from a different race, with a different language and a different culture. However, such romances require much more work. One must learn the language, the culture, and the different sexual positions used (not exactly easy to master—start researching the latest cultural trends in sexual positions!). Leaving all laughter aside, unconditional love doesn't work on a daily basis. Just the existence of the thousands of cultures that we now have proves my point—namely, generally speaking, humans stick with their own kind! Now, one might state the obvious and say that such a thing only proves that humans are incapable of unconditional love. However, my response to that is even more provocative: if you want unconditional love, then you must abandon the sexes. It is a condition when we choose to "love" someone from the opposite sex only. That's a condition. When I tell a girl that I love her, I am assuming that she is a female. I am assuming she has a vagina and a uterus (and, if I'm the lucky guy, a fresh-off-the-press set of ovaries!). However, the moment I find out that this "girl" that I "love" actually has a penis, Oh God, someone roll out the track field—I'm running!

Though I am obviously taking the extreme, I hope I am exposing, however slowly, the futility of believing and hoping in an unconditional love. What must also be considered, more seriously, are the realistic things that one engages with in the real world.

When one utters the statement "I love you unconditionally," one must seriously consider what unconditionally really means to that person. For example, when I tell a girl that I love her unconditionally, maybe that simply means that if she's going to have a bad day (or two…) I would forgive her and move on. However, if, let us suppose, that in a year she were to become insane, maybe my "unconditional love" wouldn't be a match for such a "twist of fate"? Here, we see, that every aspect must be looked at.

In a religious environment, such as within Christianity, one must assume that the other mate would remain a Christian. In order for a perfect love to continue, the husband must be Christian and so must be the wife. However, that is an absolute condition and presupposition. One cannot know whether in the next fifty years, one's spouse would remain a Christian! That's like asking the majority of Americans, who claim to be Christian, to be prophets! Prophets who would foresee the future religious state of their spouses. Such an idea is absurd. At least in Baptist circles (not in Pentecostal ones, however). We all know that religion is important. And the moment something happens religiously, is the moment something happens spiritually—is the moment something happens romantically. The couple that experiences a change in religious beliefs on one side may end up in deep trouble. Often times, we like to emphasize certain things that fit our intentions. For example, a religious advocate may state that, even with a change of religious views "unilaterally," one must maintain a state of *unconditional* love. The emphasis is on the word "unconditional." Let us suppose that a Christian wife has a husband that becomes a crazy drunkard. Let us suppose that he becomes an atheist. Now, we all know that—in the beginning—the love that existed was allegedly "unconditional." However, to be realistic, we also may note that, when the husband became a drunk atheist, the wife began to focus on the "unconditional" part of the phrase. Being a "good Christian," she would stress the term *unconditional*. However, as to the second term in the phrase—love—she would let that slide (usually—and in theory). I think that what needs to happen is a reversal of emphases: it should be unconditional *love*. However, such optimistic thinking is hard to come by. In our day-to-day life, we may stress certain things that distort the original meaning and intention. As in this case, we can have a faithful wife placing emphasis on "unconditional." But the "love" part remains silent.

I am certain that there are humans that love with a more limited amount of conditions, but not to have any conditions *per se*, is impossible. It is impossible because one must be familiar with all possible conditions in order to know if one has no conditions. (And that is impossible to know in one's lifetime. One would need a million lifetimes to determine if one is familiar with all the conditions and if one requires any.) What is striking, though, is that one never really thinks about the meaning of conditional love. What I mean is this: is conditional love really so bad. Let us suppose a scenario. I marry a girl who has certain conditions. She marries me and I have certain conditions. She requires that I make fifty thousand a year and I require that she make me Italian dishes five times a week. We get married, meet the requirements, and live happily ever after. What's wrong with the picture? Nothing. Exactly. It's too real for anything to be wrong with it! This is the sort of love that I am talking about. And it's okay to have conditions. It's okay to tell your husband that he must stay sober or you will leave him. It's okay to tell your husband that if he ends up killing your kids, you wouldn't love him. It's okay to set limits. It's okay to be human! It's normal to tell your wife that if she cheats on you, your love will decrease by an ounce. It's okay to be honest.

It is not okay to set stupid conditions. For example, it is not okay to use sex as collateral. This is so stupid and it's been used by an entire multitude of morons. It's a big no no. It's not okay to require things that are stupid. And you know if it's stupid when I tell you it is! How can you tell if it's "stupid"? If it doesn't bring about love, consider it stupid.

The greatest argument against the existence of unconditional love I have saved for last. I have ranted on and on about how such a love is ridiculous; for those who are not thoroughly convinced, I offer the best now. It is a well-known fact that what sets apart one human from another are *conditions*. One man is different in comparison to another man by a different combination of conditions. One man requires this condition, another man requires that condition. This is what sets apart humans from one another. For example, I am different from the next guy standing next to me because I have certain conditions that differentiate me from the rest of the crowd. I could, for example, become irritated when someone talks about democracy—thus, in order to make me happy, one would need to eliminate the use of that word; that would make it a condition upon which my happiness rests. Therefore, a person would have to know the conditions of my happiness and eliminate whatever it is that makes me unhappy—in this case the arbitrary use of the now-meaningless term "democracy." Another person may have different conditions. Another man may need a wife that cooks Italian dishes—his happiness rests on that. It is a condition that separates him from me. It is what sets us apart. These traits, these characteristics, these *conditions*, they make us *unique*. Conditions make us unique. They set us apart from one another; they make Moses Moses and Adam Adam. Conditions make Christ who He is. Conditions make us who we are. Because conditions contribute to our uniqueness, saying that an *unconditional love* exists for a very *conditional person* is ridiculous! We are merely things made up of various conditions! Had humans been unconditional creatures, uniqueness would cease to exist. We would not have "conditions." I would be just as happy as the next person next to me. Fred wouldn't be angry if his wife made him Italian dishes, and neither would I be angry if mine made me Mexican. We would be creatures of unconditionalism. We would be unconditional and we would love unconditionally. Every single person would be exactly the same as the next. We wouldn't have preferences. I couldn't say that Italian food makes me happy; that would immediately betray a sign of a "condition"—my wife would feel obligated to make Italian dishes. Fred couldn't become specific either, for how could he, before such a thought occurred to him, he would be labeled a conditional person. One could argue that preferences are to be kept separate from conditions, however, such is virtually impossible. In the real world, preferences *are* conditions. My preference of reading Roman history allows me to seek out a wife who is also interested in Roman history. Such a preference becomes somewhat automatically and arbitrarily a condition. Now I am seeking a wife that must meet a certain condition; namely, she must like Roman history. This is beautiful. I do not see the necessity of loving unconditionally. I think it stupid.

What I am arguing is that conditions are preferences, and preferences make us unique. They make us who we are. If conditions didn't exist, we would all cease to have an identity. You know that when you come to me, Moses, you will be met by a person who has certain conditions. You do not swear around me, you do not talk lowly of others around me, you do talk about politics and you do talk religion and relationships. These are preferences that automatically become conditions. You are coming to meet me, and I am a unique combination of conditions. These conditions determine whether you and I will have a potential meaningful friendship. These conditions make me who I am. If you don't like them, leave them. This is what makes us (and me) very human. We are conditional *by nature*.

For those who would like to talk about a potentially less conditional love, I would recommend talk of what I call *emphases of conditions*. In order for one to have a meaningful relationship, one must learn to place emphases in all the right places. For example, if my wife failed to make my favorite dish, should I be angry? According to my preset conditions, yes; however, the emphasis could be delayed at will. I do not have to be angry with anyone. I do not have to stick to my conditions always. I can have fluidity to my character. This fluidity would, in turn, also contribute to who I am as a person. Conditions are there to help establish meaningful relationships. Conditions are there because we are the body of Christ and the body is made up of various members. And these various members are us. I am a hand, you are a foot. And we serve different functions. I am a historian, you are an architect. I write a book, you design a house. I am a nurse, you are a doctor. We all serve our unique—condition-full—purpose. I argue that if one wants to have something near an unconditional love, such as a love that cares not if one's wife is beautiful or not, one must learn to be flexible. One must learn that conditions make us who we are, but they can also destroy who we are. Conditions set us apart, but conditions are like colors; they help set us apart, but no one says that we can't adapt to the environment. In winter, one could be black (to help absorb sunlight, which contributes heat); in summer, one could be white. The environment helps us choose our colors. I am arguing that conditions are a must for society to exist—however, I am also arguing that these conditions should not be set in stone. We must be flexible.

The only place where one can find some form of unconditional love is God. And how that works, I don't know. (At least I'm being honest.) I could ramble and tell you a million tales about a love that is unconditional, but with such a love I am most unfamiliar with. And neither are you.

CHAPTER EIGHT

A Flicker Then a Burn

Like most people, I've never handled being turned down well. At least I don't think that I have. I think that when you are turned down by someone who knows you intimately, it is much easier on a person. Because then, at least, you know that that other person seriously means it when they tell you that you are simply "not the one," or something as lame as "I'm sure God has someone out there for you, far better than me."

Oh please. You could have just spat me in the face instead of giving me the religious crap. I mean, do you even believe the words coming out of your mouth? I don't think so. It hurts enough when you're turned down, but even more so when the other person is trying to sugarcoat the hands of fire—the fires that are giving you the third degree burn.

Let's face it, being turned down by someone who knows you intimately isn't so bad. Sure, you know the person more and are more attached to him or her, but when they say "No," you know that that is a solid "No." There is no sign of hope for such a case. All you have to do is have the guts to come clean and walk away. And then try to forget everything. That's obviously what most of us have trouble with: we simply cannot forget. However, at the very least, you know that that person made a decision to say no for whatever reason because they *knew* you well. The word *knew* is the key word. They didn't speculate anything, they knew full well what they were turning down. Because some of us have to learn that not everyone likes us, such relationships are painful. But pain is merely weakness leaving the body. Or so they say. I think that in such a case, when someone who knows you intimately turns you down, there simply isn't much, if any, hope. It really is a matter of forgetting. And that no paper, book, or scientist can teach you. You simply must forget.

On the other hand, when you have someone turn you down who hasn't given you a chance, that hurts the most. Simply because you know beforehand that the other person had not taken the time to know you on an intimate level. And, therefore, the person is turning you down without knowing who or what they are leaving behind. And I think that all of us deserve a chance. We all deserve to be understood and accepted. Everyone needs to be given a chance to speak and to express the depths of his or her heart. And it hurts the most when such an opportunity is not given. Because then you have the existence of hope. And hope, believe me, can kill everything. Hope can drive you insane, it can make you mad; it can ruin you, it can kill you. Hope is what drives a man, and hope is what kills a man. Hope is what builds relationships and hope is what kills them. Hope is the goddess of romance and Hope is the Archenemy of romance. It is a paradox. Hope is.

It is when the man hopes that things would turn out better that he is pushed near the borders of insanity. It is when he knows that the girl who turned him down had no idea of who he really was; therefore, her "burning" him is rendered useless—it is rendered inadequate as a reason because she had not known what she had turned down. In such a case, there is still hope. Of course, if one or the other still pursues the relationship.

The guy may be turned down too soon in the relationship only to be given a chance to express his true inner-self later on and have that relationship reestablished and the "turning down" annulled. All because of hope. The guy sits there and reasons with himself: Sure, she turned me down, but that's because she hasn't given me a chance and hasn't gotten a chance to know me. Maybe if she knows me on a more intimate level, she may even fall in love." Such is the state of the hopeful mind. It is the most horrible, goddamned thing in the world to have a hopeful mind. It is utterly depressing, futile, passionate, romantic, hateful, bittersweet and yet the most beautiful thing in the world. For a strange reason, the hopeful mind conquers all—it rises above its antagonists—hate, miscommunication, lack of communication, etc.—with absolute vengeance. And conquer them all it does.

Surely it's a strange sight to see a girl and guy back together after the fight. Those words "after the fight" almost always are followed by "hope." Something about hope that gives the couple the strength to continue—no, even the *need* to continue. Hope is really why the couple is back together: they have somehow realized their inadequacies as human beings and have realized that, potentially, change can occur. Thank you, hope.

And yet hope is what kills me. I don't want to have hope. I pray on a daily basis that it is taken from me. Why be frustrated? Why think about some relationship that *has no hope?* It battles me that I carry this hope within me. It'll be the death of me. I really don't want to have hope anymore. Anything but hope. Give me peace, give me love, but take away all the hope that I have. Take it away.

And then what? Then what? Without hope, what's the point of anything and everything? Without the hope of having a family, what is the point of marriage? Without the hope of having children, what is the point of sex? Without the hope of making life better, what is the point of life? Without the hope of having nutrients feed your body, what is the point of eating? Hope.

Give me my hope back.

And yet, I still feel hope burning within me—first a flicker then a burn. It is a fire that rages on within me;

unquenchable, unchanging, unrelenting, unstable, and absolutely ferocious. And yet this fire is what quenches all other fires—the fires of doubt, the fires of futility. Hope is surely an odd commodity.

My problem with hope, at the moment, is that it is ruining me. Instead of trying to pursue a relationship with her, I should have sat by and not done anything. I should have just let everything slide. So what that she didn't give me a chance? So what that she cares not? So what that she refuses to allow me to speak my mind? So what that she never replies to anything I think or say? Who cares? Really?

Hope has become my enemy. The enemy. I don't enjoy its presence under the shelter of my heart. I'd prefer that she never writes back. She never will, anyways. I think that I am rather certain that she never will. And that is what hurts me the most. Maybe if she'd just tell me that I am a horrible person, it would make things so much easier. At least then I would not have hope. But neither would I care about her comment. For I know that that is simply not true. I know how to take care of a girl and how to treat one. And that is a certainty. But she wouldn't want to test me either. For she has refused to offer me a chance. She has nothing to lose… and yet, she loses. But what she loses is whatever she put in. And that hardly amounts to anything at the moment. Which is why she won't feel anything. She has sheltered her little heart from anything and everything. As if love requires of her to be sheltered. I highly doubt that love requires anything. So long as she keeps herself safe, so long will someone else misunderstand her intentions. And they are good intentions. Of that I am particularly certain. I do not, by any means, see her as a bad person. God forbid if I said anything bad about her. She is a good person. But as with all good people, there are flaws. But I don't care for them.

Since she won't respond to me, I know there is no hope. And that is a certainty. If there is one thing I learned from her, it is this: she won't respond. And because I have always been bad at taking in what I have termed "ignoring bliss," I know that it is really what hurts me the most. But because I have experienced all of this before, on a much larger scale, I suppose that I will survive. Until the next girl I meet who pulls a cold shoulder. And then it will be the same thing all over again, except this one will have a different face and a different name. But I shouldn't be too concerned, for if I had no hope, I would be a heartless bastard. I wouldn't care for the damage done—implied or not implied, intentional or unintentional—so long as I continue to be a human being. So long as I continue to have some sort of pity and compassion in me, that will be enough. I don't think that I am much of a person who flirts with hurting the feelings of others, I have never been good at it either. Of course, there are always those moments when you say something that you've never truly meant, or those times when something you've said was misunderstood. In spite of it all, never was I one to be cruel and calculating. Most of the time, everything that was ever spoken by me that was evil was in the heat of the moment. And that doesn't count. Or at least it shouldn't. Nonetheless, even factoring in any sporadic and highly-packed moments, for the most part, I've learned not to let anything consume me or make me angry. So far as I can tell, I haven't been angry for the longest time ever. Anger is, in my opinion, just futile. But enough about me.

At the moment, I am at peace with myself. *I have learned not to be angry with anyone and I have learned what it is to be utterly burned. Instead of being an acute pain, it now has become the dull and chronic beating of my heart.*

CHAPTER NINE

Colors

Rose colors say so little about anything worth saying. And yet, somehow, if one can properly define the colors, the rose takes on a new life—it bears weight and carries with it new meaning. I wanted to define my own colors. I wanted to allow roses to say what I have always wanted them to say; I wanted them to say what I have always thought of saying but somehow never said. Roses: silent words of the unspoken. Or maybe roses say what you were never allowed to say. Maybe the colors have a deeper meaning to them. I don't know, for me, roses need to say something in particular, not something totally vague. I think that only particular statements are of any true value. It is not enough to call a woman simply "beautiful." It's not enough to say something as unsubtle as that. *A woman loves to be defined, not generalized.* Anything can be beautiful. This writing could be called beautiful. The roses could be called beautiful. If the colors take on meaning—specific meaning—then the words that were never spoken take on meaning. And if the words take on meaning, then the woman is no longer being generalized. Such is the state of colors. If I could somehow communicate what I had wanted to say with colors, I would do it with roses. If I wanted to say something to a girl that was worth hearing, it would have to be specific—not general. Something as mundane as "beautiful" is essentially lacking in zeal and passion. It is not specific and neither does it bear much significance. However, if I, somehow, have defined the colors and somehow elaborated on their meaning—specific meaning—the roses would actually say something to a particular person at a particular time. It is much better to be specific, nobody likes to be thrown into a category—such as "beautiful—and then systematically labeled, almost heartlessly. The individual—the woman, in this instance—wants to remain unique as a human being. And generalizations destroy that uniqueness—thus destroying meaning. For example, if I gave orange roses to a girl, she may read them as saying that she is "desirable"— for such is one of the meanings of the orange rose color. But what does it mean to be "desirable"? Anything can be "desirable." One may desire water when one is thirsty. Is the same "desire" felt for both? I think it necessary to define colors, then; and not only necessary, but vital. It would be more superior for each individual to define his or her own rose colors. It would be more delightful to give a girl deep, red roses and have them uniquely defined. Then those roses would take on a meaning that is specific, unique, and directed at one, single, particular person at a particular place. I could, for instance, give red roses to a girl and express in one way or another that deep red, for me, means this form, or this sort, of a particular "passionate expression." I would define passion with myself in such a way that the significant other would clearly understand the meaning of the color(s).

If rose colors bear meaning, they must have some sort of specific meaning. I could, for example, give a lime rose to a girl and define that color not to mean "plenty" and "fertility," but how these roses remind me of the color of her gorgeous eyes. In this sense, do I argue for the specific definition of rose colors. (However, I do understand that most men are not interested in defining rose colors. So I doubt that many men will actually go so far as to define rose colors when they hardly ever give them to their loved ones. Nonetheless, I am concerned about setting particular definitions for particular rose colors.)

With this new meaning in mind, the girl receiving the lime-colored rose from me would take it to mean that I have "thought" of her—thought of her eyes. In other words, the rare green rose would represent "thoughtfulness" and "remembrance," etc., when being given by me to her. (And here the particular person must be kept in mind. For if I were to, theoretically speaking, give the green rose to my sister on her wedding, it might mean a "blessing of fertility." Thus, particularities must be kept in mind.) I hope that I am somewhat making sense to the reader.

The reason I have become preoccupied with thinking about roses is because I have given roses not a few times in my life. In retrospect, I have asked myself what roses meant to females. Because I seek to understand anything and everything, I have found it necessary to think about the meaning of something as grand and wonderful as rose colors. I don't have a favorite rose. I like so many roses that it would be impossible to list them all. For scent, I have always preferred the aromatic "The Blue Lady"; for majesty, I have somewhat been attracted to the lime-green (Amandine) rose ever since I laid my eyes on it. In such a way, my mind has settled on the idea that rose colors should be defined. Everything that is worth giving is also worth considering (and retrospection on rose colors may be a considerate way of doing the "thinking").

In my own opinion, rose colors cannot be understood unless the person giving them is understood. And here lies the greatest challenge. For it is a certainty that I am most misunderstood by the general population. In fact, as Kierkegaard somewhat wittingly once remarked, even when I tell people that they do not understand me, they misunderstand me. Thus, when giving roses, I am, to an extent, being misunderstood. So, the question lies here: if one wishes the roses to have meaning, one must define them in such a way that they have meaning—but along with that, one must define himself and be understood.

Rants on Love

I think that deep red roses symbolize infatuated, absolute, romantic, exhilarating passion. A passion that is mindless and mad. That is my own personal definition of the deep red rose color. The white rose, for me, symbolizes serenity, peace, patience, and purity. It could also mean something theological, but I have not yet decided that. The yellow rose has always meant friendship, joy, laughter, happiness, and mutual attraction, for me. The orange rose meant something like the yellow rose, except that it also meant something "playful"—a friendship that is easygoing, lighthearted, and delightful. The blue and purple roses, for me, have always been primarily used simply for aromatic purposes. In giving them to someone, I would think that they would mean something about a relationship that is becoming somewhat "serious." At least that is what I think. The pink rose means something along the lines of "It's a girl" to "admiration," "grace," and "gentleness." Anything along the lines of joy and lighthearted love goes well with pink. It is a smooth and gentle color.

It has been said that in the olden days *lover birds would exchange more roses than they would words*. The rise of feminism—which ushered in the death of absolute chivalry—brought about the annihilation of roses and the rise of words—but even those words were mostly curse words. I think that it is a good thing that the ancients saw the significance of the rose. It is, sadly, something that is becoming more and more irrelevant with each passing day.

Romantic courtship included the use of roses as a substitute for the use of words—but since we have no more courtship today, along went the roses.

I send out rainbow bouquets when words have, in some odd way, escaped me. I think the combination of rose colors gives the receiver the understanding that what the giver wanted to say is simply…everything. I send out "rainbow bouquets" when what I should have said was somehow either misunderstood or left unsaid. For if I were to simply send a deep, red rose, maybe I have missed the joyful presence of the yellow rose? Maybe what the receiver wanted was joy—and not simply passionate romance. And had I sent out simply a yellow rose—as symbolic of friendship—maybe the receiver wanted something more than simple acquaintance? It is these so-called "maybes" that have me baffled. It is why I think that the rainbow bouquet is perfect for any occasion.

I am now sending a rainbow bouquet, or at least I hope to. I send roses when I feel like doing it—not out of pressure, but out of cheerful giving-ness. Someone once said that God loveth a cheerful giver. It is why I like to give things when I am cheerful. I think that the variety of colors expresses whatever had needed to be expressed—and most of my feelings are ambivalent; which is why I prefer the rainbow bouquet. There's something about sending roses that gives me peace—though the roses will most likely not mean anything to the girl I am now sending them to.

But, to me, they will have meaning. It is better to give than to receive.

I used to give roses to girls and expect something in return—it was a selfish gene. No longer do I think that way—or, at least, I shouldn't. I give roses because in giving them I have somehow expressed myself in a more fuller manner; I have somehow spoken the unspoken. It's as if a weight had been lifted off of me. I like to set things right with people. And when I send roses to a girl, it gives me a sense of being at ease. It gives me a sense that everything will be fine—whether she accepts my roses or not. Whether she thinks they are worthy of bearing meaning is entirely up to her, she could accept them as such or she could redefine them in some other manner—absolutely defacing them of the meaning I have given them. Being ever hopeful, I do hope that the receiver receives my roses with a sense of joy and at least some inner peace. I would like for the girl to feel that. If she does not like my roses, I hope that she forgets me and simply redefines their meaning into something more tangible and pleasant to her own tastes. That is, if she does not like my roses. On the other hand, if she accepts them—and I do hope that she does—I hope that maybe they will have meaning for her. *Meaning is everything.*

When she receives my roses, I will not say anything—those who seek, will find. If she wants an answer, she can always find it—for she already holds the answer, she just needs to discover it. Neither will I leave a note. Notes just destroy the purpose—if you are intending to speak without the use of words, then the use of words (in a note attached to the roses) would merely destroy the entire purpose of the roses. Therefore, I think roses must be kept separate from notes.

I do not think that she will accept my roses. Which is why I am giving them cheerfully. To give or not give, that is not a question I face. Rather, to give with the idea of receiving instant response or to give with the idea that I will get no response—not even a thank you—is the real question. I think it is the latter. However, I will not trouble myself, so long as I did what I feel is right. As for the rest, the rest the girl can decide.

As for my readers, go out and discover your own colors. Find whatever it is that has meaning and redefine it. Rose colors have an unspoken language. *Find your colors.*

CHAPTER TEN

Afraid to Love?

"To love at all is to be vulnerable. Love anything and your heart will be wrung and possibly broken. If you want to make sure of keeping it intact, you must give it to no one, not even an animal. Wrap it carefully round with hobbies and little luxuries; avoid all entanglements. Lock it up safe in the casket or coffin of your selfishness. But in that casket—safe, dark, motionless, airless—it will change. It will not be broken; it will become unbreakable, impenetrable, irredeemable. To love is to be vulnerable"

—C.S. Lewis,
The Four Loves

For all of Lewis's wisdom, this saying alone qualifies to be placed in the Holy Bible. I have not personally encountered a more poetic (and truthful) description of what it means to love another human being. *It is a certainty that love involves uncertainty.* Love is something that just happens, and it is something that is meaningful. But even with chance, love is not chance *per se*; love is a choice. Only in that casket or coffin could a person become so detached from society that he could, theoretically, never learn to love. For how could he? He surrounds himself with nobody he could love. For love is a risk, and that risk he does not want to pay.

It is a horrifically sad place to be. For the person feels as if to love would be some undeniable pain—but to *not* love would be a pain that is chronic, a pain untreatable by modern medicine. Love has always been a risk. To love someone else is to expose the very secrets of your own heart—it is to write letters that speak volumes about who you are. Love presupposes a certain amount of graceful fellowship. You cannot find love—or be loved—in isolation. Such a thing is impossible. And how many of us love to be isolated. We just find it amusing to push whoever it is away so that our hearts could remain safe, intact, and well-protected—but oh-so-cold. In fact, our hearts become irredeemable. No longer could we love another. For how could we cross the walls that we ourselves, with our own hands, have built up for so-called shelter and protection? Those walls are unbreakable. Such walls are built up of many things— we could surround ourselves with cute, little hobbies and wonderful little church groups. We could surround ourselves with armchair theology and lock our study room from the rest of the world. In fact, we could be saints and Christian missionaries while building those very (cold and cruel) "walls of protection." Those walls are indestructible and impossible to leap over—even an assault such as an absolute siege would probably be of no benefit. How could one save someone who has already *saved* himself? (For he already built his walls, his temples, his coffins that shelter his unreachable heart.) Hardly does the person stop and think about what exactly it is that he is sheltering himself from. You are saving yourself from…? From what? Love? You build walls and destroy fellowship so that love may have no chance of occurring? Is that really the meaning to life? I think not. Love is essentially found in communion. And we establish that close association only by communicating with one another. Sharing our thoughts with one another over and over again. Those who are afraid to love have trouble with communicating. They have trouble with a lot of things; but those troubles, they are merely reflections of what truly lies at heart: the fear of love. No, not merely fear, but the necessity of being afraid of love—afraid to love and to be loved. But even here I am not correct, for they want to be loved. But who can love someone stuck in the cold of a coffin? Does one have access? It is like a lock that has no key—one who is afraid to love simply gives nobody access. They hide under platitudes and sulk when love is mentioned. For they will make up anything to make sure that their hearts are safe, secure, and impenetrable. Such is the state of those who are afraid of love. Their motto is: avoid all entanglements. Refuse to associate with people, refuse to allow yourself to be loved. Refuse to be yourself in public. In the open. Refuse to reveal the desires of your heart. Refuse. Refuse. Refuse.

And eventually the world does refuse: it refuses *you*. People stop believing in you. For how can they? For them, you no longer exist. You are dead. Remember that coffin you placed your cold and safe heart in? Sure, it was safe for eternity, but nobody could love it. Nobody could penetrate whatever secrets it contained. But nobody tried. You know why? Because people ceased to care about the one who ceased to care about them. It was an eye for an eye in the real world. Go ahead, lock yourself up. Hide your face from society and find comfort in hobbies. Those hobbies could be anything—they could be church-related or atheist-related, but so long as they keep you from loving and being loved, so long will God see them as sins. There is absolutely no use trying to fight love. It is pointless and it is futile. Love involves pain. It always had. It involves risks that are unavoidable. You could fall in love with me today and I could die from a massive heart attack tomorrow. Love involves uncertainty. It involves things that we wish hadn't existed. But love comes prepackaged with things none of us dare talk about. But someone must. And C. S. Lewis has.

I have chosen a different path. It is a path, I think, worth walking upon. Every relationship is open to the idea of love, for me. For why should it be otherwise? You suffer your pain for a day or two, and eat a jar of chocolate ice cream to comfort yourself, but at least your heart remains open to love. It remains alive. It is like a garden that is blooming. And, ever so often, someone comes in and tills the ground. Though there is pain during the tilling, however, not to worry, the garden only increases in beauty. So it is with love. Those moments of irrefutable pain and hurt are incomparable to the joy that love can potentially bring. There is no use in hiding. There is no use for me in keeping myself and my thoughts a secret. *I prefer to be an open garden to the world. Come what may, so long as you enjoy the beauty within.* Whatever beauty you may find, thank the tillers. Thank those who, unknowingly, have tilled my soils until they have become fertile enough to bring life to these exotic flowers.

I prefer not to lock myself up. I see no point in it. Along with C. S. Lewis, I think that those who are afraid of love are simply mistaken. I cannot point out their flaws, I can only set them an example. May the fruit from my own garden of love remain pure and satisfying. I seek no other option.

CHAPTER ELEVEN

Pajamas, Grandmas, and Dating Jesus

Only Moses could walk around in pajamas, talk to freethinking philosophers, argue with theologians, talk about the Virgin Birth, flirt with the cute girl at the coffee shop (being flatly turned down!) all in a matter of minutes. But even such people have problems.

For one, cute girls at the coffee shop don't care about whether Jesus came from Mary or from the *other* Mary; in fact, so long as He came from Heaven, then everything is okay. The Holy Spirit did it. Two, most people don't care if you're cool and wear pajamas. In fact, what do pajamas have to do with the Virgin Birth? Exactly. Three, why in Frankenstein's name would you be talking to brainwashed, freethinking philosophers *if* you're flirting with cute girls? And, on top of that, why quote Scripture in the middle of hot pursuit? (I mean "hot chick pursuit," of course.)

Believe me, in my dreams, I ask myself those same questions. Why theology when you can be talking sexology?

Why the Virgin Birth when you can be having fun *making that future birth happen*? Of course, we usually don't like to involve the Song of Songs when doing religious studies.

My problems all began when I became interested in politics. I wanted to infiltrate society with some good old "cleansing factors." But to do politics, one must be devoted to the *thing* politics tries to control: people. Old fashioned *homo sapiens*. Society and politicians go hand in hand. Just like Jesus and the Virgin Birth. You can't have one without the other; either Jesus was born of a Virgin Mary or He was *not* born at all. You see, the problem isn't so much that I am bad with people—in fact, I've been told that I'm quite good, *very* good—it's that I suck at doing politics the politically-correct way. And this whole politics thing isn't just about me and the One World Government—it's about me and the girl next door. I mean, how are you supposed to communicate highly-condensed, intellectually-charged philosophical formulas into a girl that is drop dead gorgeous? You can't, in theory, expect to get beauty and brains. It's like trying to get both a Muslim slut and a Christian nun all in one package. It simply cannot be done. Or so I was told. By my freethinking philosophers, of course. (I never really did figure out whether they called themselves "freethinkers" because they freely chose to think or because their thinking was *free*; namely, priceless.) I experienced a crash in my thinking. Some computer geeks would call it a "glitch"; my fellow male nurses would call it a "brain fart." Whatever you will, I was stuck counting the infinite numbers that occurred after 3.14 *pi*. My mathematically-logical brain would never solve the *pi* problem nor would it ever figure out the correlation between beauty and brains. (There is none.)

One of my sophisticated friends is a wannabe marriage and family therapist. His problems are closely related to mine: he is an unmarried, single bachelor who does not have kids. (Emphasis on "bachelor," "single," and "unmarried.") Unfortunately, he is also an uncontaminated Christian virgin practicing abstinence until marriage—or so I think—just like me! So here's Pandora's Box, which contained the following question: how does a single, virgin guy, with no kids, teach married people, sexually active, with children, how to solve problems?? I mean, isn't that like the greatest paradox of the century? Why didn't the freakin' Pharisees pose *that* question to Jesus?

Only recently have I realized that I am both screwed *and* in bad hands! Goshizzle dang it! What do you do when theology is coming out of your ears and love songs are pouring out of your mouth? Err…that was a bad analogy. Correction: love songs pouring forth from the lush, romantic gardens of my tropically-exotic heart. There. That sounds better. I was so busy trying to be poetic—and I am a poet—but I forgot that this is a theological writing being presented to my boring, old professor at Yale who teaches Pauline Eschatology 525. But I was not turning in a paper, or was I? And you, the reader, have a fat chance at getting theologically brainwashed reading my mundane ramblings. So beware. Boo.

Back to my friend—the soon-to-be-famous sex therapist, marriage therapist, family therapist, kid therapist, whatever therapist—who isn't married and who has no children. I assumed, for a while now, that I was in good hands. For the longest time, I thought that beauty and brains go, to an extent, hand in…foot. But even hand in foot wasn't so bad, right? At least all of the body parts are there…or so I thought…

Nonetheless, I realized that relationships, politics, and beauty had almost *nothing* in common. Beauty is for the front page of *People* magazine; relationships are for grandmas and grandpas; and politics is for people who don't know how to interact with people—so they theorize about how to do that all day long.

My friend, the marriage therapist, was in the same boat as me. He didn't know if he was going to get married— ever—nor did he know if he really liked girls that much. I mean, once you know everything about those creatures, don't they sort-of become boring to you? At least, that was my theory. I had many more theories, of which, I am sure, the cute girl next to you—yeah, the one reading that relationship cure book—is currently mulling over. Umm, where was I? Oh, yes, my friend and how he likes pajamas or… Wait, that was me in the pajamas. (He's not that cool…

yet.) Anyways, my friend basically cracked the female mind. (With my help, of course.) However, we are stuck now: what do we do with the leftovers? (The things left after you "crack" the nut…) He thinks that females need to be won with patience, I, on the other hand, argue for a solid ride-in: Enter Prince Charming. He is overly the "patient" sort, while I am the "zealous" and "passionate" sort. I'm the one who rushes into the games really fast.

I think that a Prince must be both competent and confident; he must ride in with force and beauty. And patience is totally not cool. A gentleman knows his place and must carry some weight of authority. Oops! I forgot that the women's rights movement passed through post-modern America. Nevertheless, a man gets the girls with brilliance.

The problem is that I tried my "brilliance" out in the real world. And, to be blunt, it was a horrible nightmare. (Except that it didn't happen at night.)

It was wonderful summer morning, the sun was shining, the birds were chirping, and on the computer was Moses sitting, talking to some cute girl on Facebook, in his white Hanes underwear (borrowed, of course, from Dad). (If you can't fill your Dad's shoes, you will never fill his underwear!) I was all grown up now and I was experiencing life firsthand.

Out there, in the cold desert lands of Facebook, I was, like a Vietnam soldier, zooming in on my target. The situation was horribly bleak, but, since I had a name to live up to (Holy freakin' Moses!), I was giving this my best shot. So, one comment after another I got a girl's attention.

And this is where the story gets bad. Wince. I got a little bit *too much* attention.

My dear friend, the marriage therapist, told me not to do this. I mean, what's wrong with telling a girl that she is pretty, right? Harmless. Sheesh.

No. Not really. Because, you see, girls raised in America are different than the rest of the human species populating Planet Earth (aka Pangaea). Girls, here, in this country, don't like compliments. They think that one-night stands do not invade personal property, but compliments do. (I miss the days when the man asked for the daughters hand from the father.)

I wish Jesus were here. He would figure something out with all of this gibberish.

Oh, yeah, the ending of the story— I forgot to state the obvious—I even gave it a new name: Facebook Divorce. It's like divorce except between so-called Facebook "friends." Oh well.

I guess the marriage therapist was right: don't even click "like" on some of these females who put pictures on Facebook.

(Note to Male Facebook Users: If the picture contains a male in it, don't click "like," you will be called a homosexual; if the picture contains a female, don't click "like," you will be labeled

a stalker; if the picture contains someone younger than 18, definitely DON'T click "like"—even if it's your own kid—you will be labeled a pedophile. Welcome to postmodern American culture: where you are guilty until proven innocent.)

Except for all of those girls who find the Facebook "like button" atrocious, most women like it. Therefore, if the stakes are high, the pursuit is worth it: go get 'em! (I am kidding.)

My friend was right, but only to an extent: who wants a relationship with an over reactive and paranoid lady? Exactly. (All of a sudden it matters not if she is beautiful-ish.)

Anyhow, when all is said and done, there still remain leftovers. Is communication really the key to a successful relationship? Is differentiation the real thing? Self-validated intimacy better tasting than other-validated intimacy? Is sex really possible for a nun?

Except for the last question, we still had plenty of "leftovers" left after we "cracked" the female mind—which means, in other words, that we never really cracked it in the first place. But it was a good feeling when maintaining our illusion (or delusion, if you will).

As for my friend, I have no doubts about it: marriage will happen. Between him and Christ, of course. As for me, well, would you, the reader, have any doubts about it? I mean, look at this horrible writing I wrote and keep in mind my politically-incorrect ideas. Choose your answer wisely.

Rants on Love

Would someone really date a theologian? Would someone really date someone who is pro-life, anti-homosexual-everything, anti-contraceptive, and pro-happiness? No, of course not. But, speaking theologically, I've had the hottest date ever: Jesus. And, guess what, who wouldn't want to date Jesus.

… Like, this one time, I take Him to Olive Garden and we choose a table that is right across from Bill Gates and his wife. Bill is busy paying the huge bills for his dinner and his drinks. We, on the other hand, sit down and order water—get this—H_2O. So they bring the glasses of water over and BAM! Jesus turns them into fine Italian wine and then He… (…and so the story continues…)

CHAPTER TWELVE

Questions About Love

Plato wrote this phrase many times: ΓΝΩΘΙ ΣΕΑΥΤΟΝ ("know thyself"). I have spent most of my life being honest with myself—along the way discovering and rediscovering myself. Nothing sounds more reasonable than knowing myself. I am taking Plato's advice seriously; I am thinking about myself and my own relation to that abstract thing called love. Every once in a while, I find myself staring into the eyes of somebody I find interestingly appealing. Whenever I have any sort of feeling or thought about somebody outside of my own neuronal existence, I immediately begin dissecting myself. I cannot help but attempt to understand myself— what is it that I am seeking? what is it that I am seeing? what is the meaning of this? I ask myself questions so that I may come up with answers—in the process, I find myself beneath the encrustation of my own existence. Living in the question is the answer. By *living in the question*, I find myself. I shed all that which entangles me. If living in the question is important, then asking the right questions is proportionally important also.

So when I meet a girl I am attracted to I have usually two questions for myself: (1) is this merely physical and meaningless; or (2) is this spiritual and beneficial? Most of the time I relegate all of my so-called feelings to the dustbin of useless and meaningless lust; this form of attraction is nothing more than photon-dropping, photoreceptor-stimulating, hormone-aggravating illusion. Everybody does it. And I am not everybody. Which means that this form of attraction is not me or myself—it belongs to the Nietzschian "herd," to the rest of the world. Anybody is capable of "falling in love" with photoreceptor-stimulating beauties. But not everyone is capable of actually loving. In fact, most people are incompetent lovers. So the question that I ask myself is: is this attraction merely to be attributed to fluctuating hormones and materialistic notions of being *or* is this something else? (Most marriages are based on materialistic notions of "being," that is, marriages are based on empirically materialistic factors like physiology, which are then used to create a sense of "being" based off of nothing but hormones, pheromones, and lust.)

Most of the time, I answer my own questions. Sometimes, however, it is more complicated. I ask myself only to be baffled. I find that I cannot answer my own questions. In such a moment of honest paradox, I find myself coming truly to life. I begin to wonder about I. When I am attracted to a girl for all of the right reasons, I usually find myself coming up with reasons to criticize my own attractions. (One never knows how far a philosophical thought can take one.) I like to take the philosophical journey often. When I am in such a state, I question myself and submit my feelings and thoughts to a form of self-examination that involves brutal honesty. I find myself questioning everything—even myself. Sometimes I wonder if it gets the best of me. (Which it does.)

When I move past the first question and begin entertaining thoughts about the second question, that is when my guard is most up. Is this attraction more than merely fluctuating feeling? Is this attraction completely independent of hormonal and pheromonal fluctuations? Is this attraction based on friendship and predestined commonalities? If so, then maybe this "spiritual stuff" cannot be scrutinized using "empirical" methods. Maybe true love falls outside the limits of reason. Maybe an elusive love is so because it *is* love. Maybe a love that cannot be reasonably (sic) criticized is actually the only form of (abstract) love. It makes me recall a story one of my professors once reported about another colleague.

Once upon a time there was a twenty-something year old boy who met a girl at his university. He met her as he was walking up the steps leading to one of the halls. It was love at first sight. Within a few years, they were engaged and were sitting at a fancy restaurant planning their wedding. When all of a sudden, the boy (now a man) pulled out a piece of paper on which he had written all

Rants on Love

of the empirically reasonable reasons for reasons pro and con regarding their engagement. He determined, using a simple empirical method, that their engagement was not "reasonable." He showed the girl his paper and she read it. She saw that he had listed much more things on the "con side." She carelessly brushed it aside and stated matter-of-factly, "Don't be silly, we're getting married." And they lived happily ever after.

Using logic and reason, one would assume that such a move on the part of the girl would be fatal. Fortunately, it wasn't. They did live happily ever after. The question is: why did the boy choose to ignore all of the "reasons"? Why not go ahead with *reason* and ignore *heart*? Why should love be irrational? (In fact, is it?)

For those of us who aren't religious, there is no such thing as love. In fact, there cannot be such a thing. Love is dismantled and reduced to nothing but adrenaline, oxytocin, a couple of aromatic pheromones, and a lot of sex. It is reduced to all things empirical. In fact, love has a very articulate anatomy that can be described and catalogued.

But for those of us who like to ask bigger questions—which came first, the chicken or the egg?—we simply choose to believe in the realm of the spirit. Something divine makes it all sound reasonable. For those of us who like to think critically, we see the problems with empiricism and we see the problems with irrational spiritualism.

Nonetheless, we conclude that there is something bigger than hormones and lust involved here.

I've made a choice a while back to accept the fact that love cannot be catalogued. Love cannot be reduced to words. Love should not be reduced to words. You should not merely say "I love you"; your entire existence should breathe love into every sphere of your beloved's life. You should not dissect love and dismantle it into a loveless pile of technical jargon and empirical atoms. Love should remain elusive—even for the philosopher. It should remain even when all other questions have been answered. Love alone shall reign as god of questions. Love will remain a mystery that baffles the wise and irritates the stupid. It will give men suffering from erectile dysfunction four-hour erections and women suffering from sterility pregnancies. Love should remain a verb. It should not be talked about much—it should merely be the very essence of our existence. Like oxygen, it must remain a given—something no one dare mention, but something all of us could not live without, even for a second.

Whenever we cannot explain ourselves and our actions; whenever we feel as if we are insane, that is when we are closest to love. Like the father who eagerly awaits the return of his prodigal son in the parable of Jesus, we, too, must leap for joy at such a ludicrous sight—the sight of an inexplicable prodigal returning.

Concerning love, I have nothing to say.

CHAPTER THIRTEEN

Love Score: How to Measure Love

Pitirim A. Sorokin first demonstrated that human love—whether romantic, brotherly or friendly—could be measured. Though love is extremely abstract and not palpable, it can be calculated. Sorokin identified five ways for measuring love:

(1) Intensity
(2) Extensity
(3) Duration
(4) Purity
(5) Adequacy

According to the five-point measurement, Sorokin wished to eliminate the belief that love cannot be measured or objectively analyzed. Love can be analyzed somewhat objectively and anyone can "test" his or her own love—whether that love is for mother, father, sister or lover.

The first point that Sorokin made was intensity. Love can be measured by calculating its intensity. On a personal level, for example, I can measure my love for a girl by comparing it to love that I have (or feel) for others. For example, I can compare my feelings for the girl with previous feelings for either another girl or someone I also love(d). In comparing the two, I could scientifically see whether my love is more intensive for this girl. I could weigh all of my thoughts and feelings and actions and see if they amount to more than any previous "love." In this way, I can measure the intensity of love. On a more precise level, I can calculate the average amount spent thinking about the girl. If I spend more time thinking about her than anyone else in my life, that might give me a lead. It surely suggests that, time-wise, I love her more than anyone else. I could look at actions. I could compare actions that I take to demonstrate that love to the girl. For example, if I buy her flowers every day, maybe I love her more than my mother—for whom I buy flowers once a month. Other ways of measuring intensity can be easily produced. The point is this: a person can compare his own intensity of love towards virtually any human being on the planet.

The second point deals with love's extensity. How extensive is your love? Does your love just encapsulate one person on the planet? Or does your love wrap around a million people in its arms? This point can be quite objectively demonstrated; numbers can be used. All one has to do is count friends. Sit down and count every person you know fairly well and calculate whether you love him or her.

Rants on Love

Write down the total number. For example, currently, I am "in love" with roughly 350 people. Outside of this arena, I practically love no one else. Three-hundred and fifty is my love's extensiveness. That is how extensive my love is. A solid, scientific, mathematic and objective number. This number allows us to clearly see how extensive our love really is. If you wanted to see whether your love has increased over the years or decreased, all you would have to do is compare numbers. If you loved a hundred people last year, but now you love a million, then that clearly suggests that your love has increased.

However, one quickly can see a problem here. What if I love a hundred people with an extreme intensity one year, but another year I love a million with a very mild love? Don't the numbers lie? I mean, the numbers suggest that my love has increased when it really has decreased. That is true. Which is why numbers related to extensity alone are not calculated: we calculate intensity (amongst other things). The numbers must be considered holistically.

The third point is duration. How long does your love last? Does it last a day? Two? A year? A decade? How long? This is a measurement that is also rather objective. We have concrete numbers to go by. For example, I can look at my mother and say that I have loved her for 22 years. However, when looking at my ex-girlfriend, I can assert that I have loved her for six months. When the two are compared, and the numbers are isolated, it appears that my love for mom has been greater than my love for my ex-girlfriend. In such a way, one can measure love. One can look at concrete numbers, concrete actions, and determine one's own level of love—rather, one's own *amount* of love.

The fourth point deals with purity. How pure is your love? In other words, what sort of motives do you have when you love someone else, someone *other* than *yourself*? Do you love your mother because she cooks for you and cleans? Do you love your girlfriend because Friday night sex is bomb? Do you love your husband because he is a millionaire? There are a million motives for disillusioned "love." However, *none* of them are normal or okay. They are all illusions. The only love worth considering is pure love. Love that is not bound by absolute conditions or by motives. A love that transcends such humanness. That sort of love is worth loving. Why do you love yourself? Is it because you breathe? So do others. Is it because you look good? So does somebody else. Is it because you are smart? Remember that someone also taught *you*. Is it because you are talented? So is somebody else. Why do you love yourself? There really is no reason. You just do. It's called semi-unconditional love. A love that basically has no conditions. You have no motives when you love yourself. You don't tell yourself, "I'm going to love myself if I cook for myself today" or "I'm going to love myself if I have good sex today." Such a love for self is virtually non-existent. In a similar way, one must learn to love others as one loves oneself. Which is what

Jesus taught. Except everyone has misunderstood what He said. People have never identified or confessed to loving self. We never understood what it meant, how could we do "it" to others? Love that is pure is motive-less love. Love that expects nothing in return. That sort of love is what we call pure love. And can it be measured? You bet!

The fifth and last point deals with adequacy. This is something that is rather hard to pinpoint objectively; it requires much reflection and much knowledge (and thought). How adequate is your love? For example, if my wife "speaks love" in a "different language," then my ways of showing love will never be understood by her. My love for her, as it is being expressed, will not be *adequate*. She may be a time-centered woman—she may want me to spend time with her. I may be a gift-centered lover, I would shower her with gifts. I would express my love. However, my love would not be adequate. Or, more accurately, though my love may be adequate enough, it would not be expressed in an adequate manner. In this way is adequacy "measured." One must see just how adequate one's love really is. Are people understanding you? When you bring home flowers, does your wife think "He loves me" or does she think "He wants sex tonight"? What does your wife think? How does she understand you? Does she understand you at all? How adequate is your love? Is your love being properly expressed? This is where things get a bit fuzzy. We step into the realm of differentiation. We need to be so differentiated that we can be ourselves and yet express ourselves in ways that others understand us. I can love my wife but is my love being registered as "love" on her radar? You can kiss your wife and she may think that you want sex. And you may honestly not want sex. Maybe you really just wanted to let her know that you care. However, if love is not being expressed correctly, it basically fails to have meaning. If I wrote a novel about ending war and it was interpreted as a novel dealing with the stimulation of war, isn't my novel useless? (In the sense that its originally intended purpose had been lost, nay, it had been countered!) Likewise with love: *either you express it correctly or you don't express it at all.*

There is also another aspect to adequacy. There are those parents who love their child so much that that child becomes spoiled. Why does "love" create "evil"? In fact, how can love create something contrary to its nature? Well, maybe because love is not being expressed correctly. Maybe when the child throws a tantrum, you do not give in and express "love." Love has well-marked boundaries—either it breeds love or it breeds hate. Love, when expressed wrongly, can become its own enemy. The parent that gives the child everything, creates someone who is pseudo-independent (though dependent entirely on parent), proud (gets his/her own way always), arrogant, careless (still gets what he/she wants), and loveless. So many times have we seen the spoiled brat in the family that it is basically needless for me to demonstrate this. One merely needs to look at oneself.

Rants on Love

When all of these five points are taken together and applied to one's life, one gets a sense of where one stands in relation to love. Though there are some problems and critiques that can be offered here and there, this standard method of measurement still stands. Let us apply it and see how this method works in the real world.

As I stated earlier, I love roughly 350 people, at the moment. Thus, my objective number for extensity is 350. Out of those 350, I love 25 on a "intense" level. On a scale of 1 to 10—ten being the greatest and one being the least—I love 25 people on a scale of ten (Level Ten). Out of those 350 people, I love 50 on a scale of 5 (Level Five). My love for them is relatively strong, however it is not near as strong as those 25. As for the rest, I love them on a scale of 1 (Level One). Thus, the numbers run thus:

Extensity: 350
Intensity:

(a) Level Ten: 25
(b) Level Five: 50
(c) Level One: 275.

Total Intensity: 775 (Calculate by adding total numbers of the three levels together. For example, a *Level Ten* total would be 250 (10 x 25); the total for *Level Five* would be 250 (5 x 50); the total for *Level One* would be 275 (1 x 275).

Thus run the numbers at this point. Although this is a general and simple scale, one could get more specific. One could have one hundred levels and assign each individual person a fairly precise number. However, my main purpose is to demonstrate that love is measurable.

To take this measurement further, I would need to look at my love's duration. I would calculate by number of years "in love." (If one wanted to be more specific, one could count months or days.) Out of the 350 people that I claim to love, 25 of them I have loved for over 10 years. Thus, I would assign them to the Duration Ten category. Fifty of them I have loved for five years (thus I would assign them to the Duration Five category) and the remaining 275 I have loved for a year or less (thus I would assign them to the Duration One category). The measurements would run thus:

Duration:

(a) Duration Ten: 25
(b) Duration Five: 50
(c) Duration One: 275

Total Duration: 775

Our next measurement would involve purity. I would say that I have pure love for 10 of the people in my life. The love is absolutely pure, which would place it in the Pure Ten category. Twenty would go into the Pure Five category and 320 would go into the Pure One category. The numbers would run thus:

Purity:

(a) Pure Ten: 10
(b) Pure Five: 20
(c) Pure One: 330

Total Purity: 530

Our last measurement would involve adequacy. We could similarly do what we have done for the previous points. I would assign how adequate my love is for people on a scale of 1 to 10 (ten being the greatest and most adequate form of love). Thus my numbers would run:

Adequacy:

(a) Adequate Ten: 5
(b) Adequate Five: 75
(c) Adequate One: 270

Total Adequacy: 695

At the end of our rather modest and average (inexact but decent) count, we would add up the total. For me, the **Total Love Capacity** would be 3, 125. If I am honest, and anyone else who takes this test in similar form is honest, we can then measure love systematically and rather objectively. At the moment, I can run this test on myself yearly and see if I change. Anyone can actually do this test. Due to the virtual non-existence of such tests, there is currently no human "baseline" for total love capacity. In theory, Jesus would probably be in the millions. Of course, anyone can criticize the method here and there, but the forest must not be mistaken with the trees. We are merely demonstrating that love is somewhat measurable. However off our methods may be, one thing is certain: love can be measured. And it should be. I'm running at 3, 125.

What's your love score?

CHAPTER FOURTEEN

A Philosophy of Roses

There are a multitude of reasons for sending roses. I send roses for either one of two reasons: to coax or to destroy. I send roses to either make someone fall (or stay) in love or fall out of love. In other words, roses can do more than just create relationships; they can also destroy them.

I am calling this essay *a* philosophy of roses because it is merely an examination of one sort of philosophy—and there are many other philosophies out there. It is, by no means, *the* philosophy of roses. I want that to be clear. What follows is merely my reflection on my philosophy of roses, which happens to be *a* philosophy of roses.

I recently was in love with a woman. She was very beautiful and well-mannered. She had bright, penetrating green eyes, a dark complexion, marvelous skin, and an adorable smile. I spoke with her for a number of weeks and decided that I had to either break the relationship off or take it to the next level. I was at a point in this romance where I needed to know what the girl thought of me. I was enamored by her and I found her intelligence extremely appealing. She spoke Georgian, Russian, French and English. Her English was eccentrically accented and sounded wonderful on her lips. Clearly, I had my socks knocked off.

By nature, I am an anxiously restless person. I have to know what is going on around me in order to be at any state of peace. With this particular relationship, as with many others, I had reached a point of indecision and indecisiveness. I needed to know. But I knew that I could not let her know what I was actually thinking. I needed to know if she had any affections that were eternal towards me. Something more than just the usual. I needed a sign from God. I spent a few days thinking about how to say what I felt towards her. I also knew how foolish this all was. I realized that I could not continue in this state of guessing. I did not want to spend my weeks sorting through messages sent from her and messages sent to her. I did not want to live in some sort of literary relationship. I had enough with guessing-games and I had played in the courts of literature long enough. I wanted more than the Kierkegaardian recollected moment.

So I came up with what I thought was a brilliant idea. I wanted to make her bloom. Whether she liked it or not. I was going to use shock-value to bring the princess out of her castle. It was going to be a passive rescuing.

I decided that I needed to send her flowers in order to test her reaction. Moreover, I came up with two proper responses that would occur with such a scenario: (1) if she was not committed to me, she would say "Thank you" and state that she simply did not feel the same way toward me; or (2) she would say "Thank you" and then state that it was a little too early for roses. Those were the responses that I came up with. I figured that those two would suffice. There was, in my opinion, not much room for other responses.

I felt that roses were too soon—I should not be sending them. But that was the point. In order for something to stimulate an immediate reaction, it must have shock-value. I decided that roses were going to shock her. Nonetheless, I figured that if she was committed to me, she would work around this thorny issue and merely state something like "It's too soon for roses, but thank you anyhow." In other words, I had nothing to lose in this particular situation.

But I was ambivalent. I did not know anything at this point. I was not sure if this was what I wanted or not. I was at a fork in the road—something needed to be done. It was time to either continue with the present course or jump off the ship. I decided to bring the fork closer to home. I wanted the time for decision to be here right now.

I sent her a beautiful set of yellow roses in a yellow tin vase. Attached I signed a note reading "C'est la vie et l'amour." At first I wanted to keep things simple and PG—I wanted to simply write "C'est la vie" (English translation: "Such is life"). But then I added the French phrase "et l'amour" ("and love"). Thus the message read, in translation, "Such is life and love."

Of course, I was not, by any means, in love with this girl. I was clearly on the way to that, but I had my reservations. I wanted the message to be romantic but not too romantic. I wanted to show some signs of affection but I did not want her to think that this was "crazy." I would have sent her dark, red roses had I wanted to make her feel loved. I chose yellow. I chose yellow because it is a joyful and friendly color. I did not want make her feel overwhelmed with the roses. Simply put, I did think about everything I was doing. I was formulating a philosophy of roses.

I sent her the bouquet on a Sunday. She received the bouquet at 9:08 am. Sometime around 8 o'clock she wrote me her reply to the flowers: "Obviously, giving you my address was not a good idea."

I deleted her number and her existence out of my mind immediately. There was no use pursuing her. That was the rudest comment ever made by a person who received a harmless (and gorgeous) bouquet of innocent flowers.

I never replied.

P.S. *What she doesn't know is that she fell prey to my philosophy. I knew what she would do. I wanted her to do it. Like Jesus, who was aware of Judas' betrayal, I merely nodded my head her way. I knew that I was going to be betrayed. But I wanted to leave with honor. Flowers of betrayal were as good as a kiss—a Judas kiss.*

Rants on Love

What gives me hope is that I was not outsmarted. I may have been disappointed but I was not outwitted. She may have thought that this was weird (and it was). But what she did not know is that I was aware of her response. Like a rat sitting in a Skinner Box, so was she sitting in my maze of philosophy. She could never escape, had she wanted to. However, there was freewill involved: she had all the power to either love or not love. Love was her only true option. She did not choose it. Oh well.

I suggest using this philosophy of roses to break up with a girl on good terms. Break up with roses.

CHAPTER FIVETEEN

The World in Unity (and Love)

I was thinking about the actions of others for some time now and it has occurred to me that humans lack one thing: actions. It was precisely the lack of self-initiated actions that made me realize that humans are all in the same boat together. To put it more bluntly, we are all merely *reacting* to each other; our "actions" are just *reactions* to those around us. We, alone, produce nothing. We only react. Thus, we are all together, in a sense, holding hands, and all interrelated. Each one of us reacts to something someone else either says or does; that person, to whom we are reacting, is producing actions in reaction to someone else's reactions… and so on and so forth. This world is just one huge boiling pot of humans who are reacting to one another in ways that we do not even know. Think about it: Boyfriend buys you two dozen roses, you smile, he smiles, you both are happy. Did Boyfriend act on his own? No! His action was a reaction to something you either said or did. His action was merely a *reaction*. You, in response, probably respond somehow and thus he responds to your response and the cycle continues. What's the point? Well, if we, as humans, realize how much we are indebted to one another for our very "actions," we would learn to respect each other in the strangest ways! Everything we do in life has been sparked by someone else; every thought we think, has been planted by someone else. Everything is just being borrowed, traded, passed on, exchanged, and loaned; every action we take has already been taken by someone else.

I believe such logic can only bring us to one place: love. We, out of such reasoning, may find a way to see the effects of each other's actions. Our logic would bring us to further question the importance of society as a whole. We would look at society holistically and ask ourselves what is ruining it. Knowing that every action is a reaction; knowing that every person's reaction will further inspire others to react also in similar fashion. If the reaction being produced is rather negative, the effects could be dramatic. If positive, that spark may start other fires and quickly spread. Each of us is only reacting to one another. We can see society through different lenses; we can see each other through different lenses. We might be able to understand the importance of each of us here on planet earth. If our society's status is merely a reflection of our status, should we not try to produce only the best reactions? Shouldn't we choose to respond to only the positive actions of others? (In turn, producing a wave or, better yet, a butterfly effect of positive reactions.) Our society is merely a reflection of us; not just you or me, but *all* of us. Even the most "insignificant" person is impacting our culture. Every person has the ability to produce a series of reactions. We alone choose whether we will react to the negative or to the positive; whether our "actions" will be in response to the good or the bad. We must decide. The only thing that stands in between us is us. We need to choose the good. I pray we do. And, in a sense, by realizing the importance of each one of us, maybe we could find a place in our hearts to love each other. Not out of necessity, but out of the realization that maybe our children will one day be impacted by our next door neighbor's children. If we start producing positive reactions, sooner or later, we will enter that Utopia that we have long been waiting for. Our society is just a cohesive blend of each and every one of us. Each and every trait is there. A variety of characters are mixed together and a perfect pinch of values are thrown in. And in it all we create what we call "society." I hope we can begin to realize the importance of every human. And, I hope, in some way, that we find that respect towards one another and maybe, just maybe, love.

What about actions? Are there really actions out there, in the strict sense? I have thought about that long and I have decided that science has solved the problem. Energy cannot be created nor destroyed, it can only be transferred. That sums actions up quite well. If energy cannot be created nor destroyed, and since actions are, to an extent, an outflow of energy, we can safely assume that logic and science have really answered our question. We are merely reacting. Nothing more. We are all just transferring energy and actions. We are like canals that carry water, foreign water. We are the clay in the Maker's Hand; every original action was His and His alone. Energy was created by Him. It is only logical to assume that our very first actions were also His. After that, every human reacted to the first human's actions. And the cycle never stopped. We are just carriers. Every one of us holds something and carries something that came from somewhere else. We have nothing that is truly ours. Nothing. We are all in the same boat, borrowing time and traits from each other. I think that that is significant. If we could only realize that our actions have originated in some ancient era. We would, in effect, see that we, ourselves, are really just products of society; and society is a product of God, the Initiator of the action.

There is no time to spare with such message; we must act on what we know. Maybe our lives will be changed if we'd only realize how much we need (*and need!*) each other; every one of us is going to be shaped by someone nearby. If our actions are really reactions, would not this lead us to examine the way others react to us and our own "actions"? Wouldn't we start to examine things differently? I mean, if someone punched you in the face maybe his action was not an action *per se* but merely a reaction to your stupid comments, eh? Maybe there is logic to everything. If people are merely reacting, aren't we, then, supposed to examine every one of our own actions? Shouldn't we try to understand why people react to us in certain ways? I think this leads us to Jesus' own statement—clearly paraphrased—"Do good unto others and they'll do good unto you" (Matt. 7:12). If we do good, others will, generally speaking, react to your good with goodness. We are all reacting. If so, our actions, and others' actions, are merely a reflection of us and our society.

I hope I have somehow sparked something in someone deep down. I hope that maybe we will now consider our own actions and try to align them with Universal Goodness; I hope that we realize the impact of our actions and what we leave behind when we die. *Whether we live or whether we die, our actions remain; they remain, potentially, incorporated into society, forever.* This is the thought for today. Maybe we can begin now.

CHAPTER SIXTEEN

The Sleeping Lovers

I have heard it said that life is like a box of chocolates. I don't believe that anymore. I used to. Life is a box of cheap crackers, if that. In fact, life is a box of mouse traps with rat poison. You reach in and your hands of goodness come out bruised and scarred; you do good and get stabbed in the back by those you love. Life is not a box of chocolates. I used to think that maybe we could somehow let love reign; somehow make love a universal thing. I used to believe in change. Not anymore. I used to believe in dreams; places free of any form of stupid emotions. I think only a child has such romantic visions of life. A child alone can filter out all of the negative things this world has to offer. Somehow, with age, that filter disintegrates; you lose your ability to ignore evil. You are force fed evil. On a daily basis. You are forced to eat that which is forbidden and you can't break the cycle. Sometimes, when your inner-most self recognizes the futility, you awaken and shake off this evil dream. But, before long, this futile life takes hold of you and forces you to continue with this vicious cycle; a cycle of you just laying there with this world spinning out of control. And you watch. And you think. But you refuse to take action. In fact, action is an impossibility; this world prevents people like you from living. The moment it takes notice of you, you are instantly vaporized. So you sit, and sometimes you think. We all do. I think that, sometimes, we awaken from this drunken stupor and we, for a split second, taste life and find the waters rather bitter, but we are quickly lured back to the tainted fountains of this world. No one has enough of these hypnotizing, sedating waters. And so we sleep. We are in a state that calls for attention. But no one can help, for they too are sleeping.

If only we could shake off this wine, maybe we would rise up and battle the cycle that has got us all caught up. Or maybe, the ones who fight the cycle will be labeled "heretics." They who are sleeping refuse to be wakened. We all fully know the effects of waking a drunken man from his sleep; the end result is more evil and fuss than one can handle. Therefore, we refuse to waken those who are sleeping. How could we? We ourselves are still drunk? We ourselves are still barely waking.

I have awakened. I rose to conquer, but there was no one there but myself. It is in this moment that you realize that you are the problem. The world is just an excuse that we use to cover up our own sins. "The world" is just a phrase that we use to hint that we are not the problem; the world is just a scapegoat. The evil at hand is constantly blamed on the person that is nearby. I have awakened. And I have found no one but myself there. There in the stillness I faced myself. The world continued to spin, the markets continued to be crowded. People were running around like crazy, mothers were searching for their children in the parks. Everything was still there. Only I ceased to be. For that split second, I was not one of them. Or so I thought. I was somewhere between human and spirit. I was there, in my right mind, but there was nothing to see. It was with the eyes of my inner-most self that I was watching. And I realized that we are all the same, not one iota different. You come to your senses to find out that you have no senses. You come to see the world and realize that there is no world at all.

I guess that I have somehow failed. I wanted to solve the problem. But I could not. You awaken to healing, but you fall asleep in illness. You reach out your helping hand and return with no hand at all. Goodness is being killed by Medusa. For every good deed done, two evils are committed. It's almost an endless war. I wish that I could recognize the root of the problem. That is going to take a lifetime. No need for me to deceive myself into believing that I could somehow solve the world's problems in one sitting. No need to be naïve.

The greatest problem is our refusal to solve problems. You ask those you love to talk to you and they push you way. People refuse to "create" problems. They think that by bringing the issues at hand to the surface might somehow destroy the superficial peace. We refuse to communicate to each other. We just act as if we know; as if we clearly understand. We do not. No need to lie to ourselves. We are all just ignoring the problems; we are all refusing to communicate to each other. Marriages all fail because of one thing: lack of communication. If that could be eliminated we would be living eternal bliss. Or is that also a dream?

Let us awaken slowly. If I am sleeping, would you mind waking me? It is time for us to face ourselves. There is no "world" out there. There is no carousel with others (without you). It's just you. There is nothing to see. Just listen to your inner-most self and you'll hear the words of the wise being chanted to the sound of drums. War drums. Are you in love? Are you? Prepare for battle; many battles. In fact, countless battles. From this battle, few have returned; those who have, refuse to tell the tale. They are afraid to awaken us; they are afraid that we might act inhumanly. We might, in our drunken stupor, attack those we love. And so we sleep. Who will awaken us?

CHAPTER SEVENTEEN

The Human Motive and Love

Whenever someone enters a relationship, a number of questions must first be asked—these questions you ask yourself. Every feeling of affection must be put under scrutiny and carefully examined—relationships and love are a fragile thing. Whatever it is one feels—whether it is love, sexual desire, lust, satisfaction, affection, etc.—one needs to examine oneself and wonder why such feelings (or actions) exist. Why, for example, do you feel the need to be with this person? Does this person give something to you? What is it that you are getting—if anything? What is it—if there is anything—that you are giving? Such questions, I believe, every wise person must ask himself.

I have been in love many times. It never does go well for me, but I tend to look at the bright side of things—I tend to see things a bit differently than others. I like to waste my time thinking about my own actions and why I do things. I am always questioning myself. I am too much of an introspective guy. I can lock myself in my room for weeks at a time and review everything I have done. At other times, if I am lucky, a person may join me (for example, a girl) and help me review myself (at this point, it appears, the reviews tend to become rather critical!). Nonetheless, the point is this: what are my motives when I am in love?

I remember a time when I sent a girl a single rose in a vase with a brief note. The rose was sent basically to another country, so the gift was, at least in theory, rather elegant. I had said something odd to the girl; she misunderstood me and ended up misunderstanding the misunderstanding (which is really not a good thing). Eventually, the misunderstanding became not-so-good, so I had to, somehow, apologize. In this case, my motives are relatively simple: (a) something went wrong; (b) man tries to fix it by replacing negative thinking with positive thinking via the roses; and (c) the girl can respond by accepting the gift (expression) and continue a healthy relationship. I was basically trying to set things straight. Pretty simple.

Things get more complicated when we try to identify not something as objective as the sending out of flowers. They get really complicated with love. Pinpointing what exactly love is is virtually impossible sometimes. Every human being has, to some extent, differences. We are all different from one another. It's like we are all snowflakes—no two are the same. However, as snowflakes, we do share things in common with one another: we are white, cold, and made of frozen water. However, what may be love for one person may be hate for another. One person considers it love to send a girl flowers; another person sees it as mere flattery. Thus, whenever we are "doing" love, we are engaging with some sort of unknown force (at times).

For example, when I consider dating someone, I examine my motives. I may say that I like her outer beauty. I may think that she is gorgeous, beautiful and elegant. I may find her simply attractive because of her modesty and self-respect. I may like the fact that she gets shy around me. I may find it attractive when she blushes. Maybe I enjoy her for her simplicity. I may like her cooking (who doesn't?). There are a million things that I like about her. She is tall and has gentle eyes. She likes kids (who doesn't?), she is caring and she is sweet. She understands my jokes when nobody seems to care for them. I simply need to think of her and that makes my day. I wake up to her picture hanging on my ceiling. It's all of those things.

But why me? Why do I have to be the one that is in love with her? That is the question. *Yes, Moses, you have painted a wonderful picture of this girl that you are attracted to (hey, if you don't end up dating her, leave me her number!), but please, why would she like you?* It seems that my motives are natural. Naturally, everyone is attracted to someone virtuous and beautiful. Who isn't? It appears that I may be attracted to her because my selfish self wants someone like her. Why? So I can ruin her? So I can abuse her generosity? So that I can have myself treated kindly by her on a day-to-day basis? Maybe the answer to the last question is yes.

Maybe I do want to be treated well. Maybe I will treat her just as well, but I, too, want to be treated well. In other words, I am in love with her because I am in love with myself. It appears that I want to date a girl like her because it would only benefit me and my flesh. Isn't that a selfish love? One may say that it is. But is it really?

Let us turn the tables. If it is considered "selfish" to care for one's body, than it must be considered altruistic to destroy one's body. It seems that if I want to be a "good" person, I need to love someone who would treat me bad (thus runs the logic). The absurdity of the thought should be obvious. I may want a wife that loves kids because I would only want to raise children with a woman that I both love and admire; a woman who also loves and admires me—for whatever I love in her, I will love in my children; whatever she loves in me, she will love in our children. It seems, then, necessary that two people love each other for love to work. It seems wise to love yourself and to love others.

Oddly enough, I have asked myself whether I was a selfish person. I sort of can see it, but I wanted to know just how bad it was. I wanted to see just how far I would go. Would I truly only "love" someone unless they love me? Would I really only give my best when someone else is giving me their best? Am I really like that? Is that what Jesus meant? I honestly thought about it. I really was interested in the selfishness of love. Just how dirty it can be.

Imagine that. I am attracted to this girl because she is beautiful. But what is beauty and who does it benefit? Well, me, of course! I am attracted to this girl because she is sweet. But if I end up with her, who would she be sweet to? Well, duh again, to me! It does suggest that in loving her, or being attracted to her, I am in love with myself. Huh.

Preservation of life. Sometimes I argue that that is really the case. God wants us to reproduce. And when we do have kids, God doesn't want us to hate them—for in hating ourselves we will also hate the very *replicas* (i.e., children) of ourselves. It would then seem that love is a circular thing. You get it, you give it. You give it, you get it. Come to think of it, it is sort of a nice thing. I have to admit, the system seems to have worked pretty well thus far.

CHAPTER EIGHTEEN

Existentialist Manifesto

As an existentialist thinker, I've been frequently thinking about the ethical implications that are inherently involved in the existentialist quest. Lately, I've been applying my self-asserted existentialism towards my own philosophy of ethics and my own way of life. Instead of being a theoretical philosophy, existentialism is a practical and ethical philosophy. Prior to my conscious assent to existential thinking, I was a budding existentialist; however, I am only now completely realizing what it all means for me. What is a philosophy if it means nothing to me? What is existentialism if it is mere abstract gibberish? What is Jesus to you if He means nothing for your practical life? I'm sick and nauseated from abstract philosophies. No more do I give a damn about theories and unethical paradoxes. What I care about most is the life that is not merely examined, but the life that is *lived*. I am what I am. I do, therefore, I am. I don't care about what I think. I care about what I *do*. My life is a collection of actions. It is the sum of all my activities. It is not the sum of all my

Rants on Love

thinking. As an existentialist, I find life meaningless. I seek to create meaning. But how? Some resort to some form of materialism. They worship everything that has electrons and protons. Some claim to worship spirituality and are mere materialists: the hypocritical "Christian" church is full of such people. Others, of whom I consider myself to be, are anti-materialist. We don't care about protons. In fact, we hate all that is material. What matters most to us is the heart. The friendship that lasts for no particular reason. Love that lasts because of...*nothing*. Unconditional. We believe in nothing and we worship nothing. We accept our nothingness and we accept our humanity. We assert our own humility because we find life meaningless and useless. And boring. We love because we choose to love. Unlike the hypocrites, we have freewill. We choose. I choose love on a daily basis. And sometimes I choose hate. But what I choose is entirely up to me. I am the individual. I make the decisions. What I want to do with my life is in my hands. I assert my individuality. I assert that I am a being-for-itself: I live for myself. I am not a being-for-others. I do not see myself through the eyes of a stranger. I examine my life on my own terms. Who am I? That is a question I ask and a question which I answer. I don't care about who I am according to you (i.e., others); I care about who I am *according to me*. Who is this person? When everything is tossed away, when everything is burned up and the skies are rolled up and carted away, the stars unscrewed from that beautiful sky, what remains? When humans are no longer able to judge me and I no longer give a damn about their thinking: who am I? This is the existentialist dilemma.

I've begun to live the existentialist life recently. I was in a platonic relationship with a girl and I chose to express my existentialism. I acted on my own terms. She, quite obviously, couldn't stand me. So I left. I acted. As an existentialist, I am brutally honest. I cannot lie to others. Why should I? If I lie, I am denying my own existence. I exist and I want to exist for myself. Selfish? No. I want to live an authentic life. I want to live a life where I express who I am. Where I can be myself. Where I assert myself. And if you love me, you will choose to love me for who I am. I am I.

I am not selfish. I assert my own existence because I will—along with the Kantian categorical imperative—that all humans, everywhere, at all times, should assert their own existence *genuinely*. I want humans to be themselves. To be genuine. To love with an authentic and sincere passion. To burn along with their greatest desires. I want all to live authentic lives. To choose this life. To choose their own existence. Do not choose what society tells you to choose. Do not choose what your parents tell you to choose. Assert yourself and choose for yourself. Choose wisely.

I am not speaking in revolutionary terms. I am not asking for an ugly fight. I am not defending selfish ambition and negligence of authority. In fact, I am an absolutist. I confess. I believe in God. In fact, I believe in an absolute God and an absolute authority. I believe in morality. I assert my own existence but I do not forsake God's imperatives. I am not abandoning authority.

But have I gone too far?

Not far enough.

I have chosen this life because it has chosen me. I was *damned into existence* by God and I have accepted this life. I assert myself in order to lose myself. Life is void of any real meaning. Apart from God, I am nothing. I can do all things through Him who strengthens me. By asserting myself, I am asserting God. By accepting myself, I am accepting God. What God has created, I am not neglecting. What God has given, I have received with arms wide open and a bitter heart. True, life isn't what we think it is. But it doesn't ask questions. It gives birth to you and asks questions later. I was damned into existence. So were you. Pessimistic? No, only honest. Depressing? Yes. Satisfying? Maybe.

Choose yourself.

But remember, whatever you choose, you will be held accountable on that day when you meet your Maker.

CHAPTER NINETEEN

Love, Predestined?

Is it possible for love to be somewhat "predestined"? Are people ever "made for each other"? Before we think about predestination, one must first ask if one actually has a choice *apart* from something predetermined. Do human beings have freewill? Can they actually make choices and decisions solely, on their own, apart from anyone else's input? Let us examine a number of scenarios.

I was born in February in 1990. I was born in Krasnodar, Russia. The very nature of my initial existence was ignorant of my will. For I did not *will* to be born, nor did I will anything else for that matter. I simply came into being. According to a deterministic view of things, I came into being *because of* my parents' choices. Ah! So, though I did not will anything, my parents willed something. They made a choice to have sex. The argument then goes—or so it seems—that my very first action—namely, my first breath—was merely a reaction; I was reacting to the cold air circulating around me, which was a lot colder than the temperature in the womb. My first action was, in other words, caused by my mother giving birth to me and exposing me to the cruel and cold airs of this world. Thus, my first action was merely a *reaction*. I did not *choose* to be born, neither did I *choose* to take my first breath: all of that was forced upon me, unaware of my will. (If I even *had* a will at that time!) The logic takes us thus: I was born not in synch with anything that even closely resembles *human will*. I was born because someone else wanted me to be born—namely, my parents. It follows, then, that my parents are the very cause of my existence. They have placed me here, by choice (or so I now, at this moment, think), afterward, all of my actions were merely reactions to the world they forced me into. They placed me in Russia. They made me eat certain foods. They taught me a certain language. They shaped my early years. The entire time, my *will* (if I even have one), was not once consulted. It was all done ignoring my will. My will, whatever that may be, was, maybe, not even in existence. But, by the time it came into existence (whenever that is), I made choices…but those choices, like eating chicken noodle soup at age three, were all influenced by my mother's choices—in fact, it was she who taught me and *forced* me to like chicken noodle soup. Thus, it seems that the choices I made were not my own—the will that I so desired, the will that philosophers claim exists, did not exist at all. I was just a puppet the entire time!

When, if ever, do we make decisions? When are we governed by our "freewill"? Well, someone may say that my choice to go to Barnes and Noble today was of my own liking. However, even before there was a Barnes and Noble, someone was teaching me to read books. I grew up without a TV, thus I was forced to read books. My passion for reading was *forced* upon me (and I am thankful for that— thank you very much!). I read in English. I did not choose that consciously. I was forced to go to school in Cleveland, Ohio. As a child, I hated school. That was surely *against my will*! I was taught English. I was taught to read. Did I choose that language? Did I choose to be in America? Did America choose English as its own language, or did external actions of other people—who were merely reacting to someone else's actions—choose English for America? Did those people choose English as their language, or did the language choose them? Did they will anything at all? Were they not constrained and restrained by society? Am I, too, governed by my past—which was forced upon me?

It is quite evident that others' actions influence and continue to influence me. I am not here because I chose to be. In fact, many people commit suicide because birth was completely against their will! (Sorry for the analogy.) It is quite evident that we are merely reacting to others' actions. Let us further examine my birthing scene.

One may argue that my existence began with my father and mother making *choices*—completely of their own accord. However, even my father, had he been born in America, would not have married my mother. Thus, had that happened, I would not have come into existence. In other words, my father's actions were merely reactions also. And his father's actions were merely reactions. And his father's father's actions were merely reactions, etc., etc. In other words, do humans have *actions*? It appears not. But I would like to object with another scenario.

When I walk into Barnes and Noble, I have not been predestined to be there. My mother literally forced us to love reading. My choices were limited: it was either the library or Barnes and Noble. But my choices were not controlled *per se*. I still had freewill. I could choose, of my own accord, to go to either the library or Barnes and Noble. Namely, it would thus seem, that our reactions are governed, to an extent, by our *freewill*. Yes, my mother taught me to read; no, my mother did not force me into Barnes and Noble. I made that choice myself. All by myself.

In my mind, I could have went to the local library. Both places had books. Both had books that I could read. Both had theology, philosophy, and biblical literature texts. However, I have consciously made a decision. I was *aware* of the *risk factors* for going to Barnes and Noble. I knew that it was along the path that I walked. I knew that the library was a further distance off. I knew those things. My love for coffee was inevitably given to me by my father. Thus, the café at Barnes and Noble, only coaxed me to itself more! But notice the keyword: *aware*. I was like that divine being who knows the result and action of every atom on earth—that being that knows every reaction that will follow, where each atom will eventually end up. And yet. And yet, consciously I made a decision. I could have chosen the library. I could have. I knew that coffee wouldn't be there. I could live without coffee. I have gone without it for days. It wasn't a drug that lured me. I had self-control. I was in control of my actions. However, I chose Barnes and Noble. This is complete freewill. It is freewill because I am aware of the factors that have influenced me, I am in control of the situation, I am not going against my desire or my will. I made a sober decision. I did. Not God, not Fred, not Dad, not Mom, but I. God may have influenced me. He could have increased my demands for coffee. He could have done that. He could have. But that doesn't matter, in the end, does it? I was aware that God was doing that. And yet, I succumbed. I went nonetheless. It was I who went. Not Fred, not God, not Mom, not Dad. Me. All me.

I have heard some philosophers complain that hard determinism, which argues that humans are—to some extent—not responsible for their actions, since they have no freewill, is impossible to disprove. For example, if a man walked across a bridge, a determinist would say that certain predisposing factors made the man walk across the bridge. Let us say a girl was waiting for him there. The man walked because the girl was across the bridge. However, the determinist would readily point out, the man was in love with the girl because they both lived in the same city—

Rants on Love

totally uncontrolled by both of them. (The fact that they grew up together, in the same city, may have been caused by both of their parents' "independent" decisions.) Thus, it would seem, that the man and girl were in love, not out of their own freewill, but because they were somehow predetermined to be together by other factors—not within their own control. However, had the man decided not to walk across the bridge, the determinist would argue that certain factors determined the man's actions. The problem, other philosophers point out, is how can this be *disproven*? What would it take to prove determinism wrong? (The answer is: nothing. Since any action that results is already alleged to be a reaction, not an action *per se*.) It reminds me, again, of the "little, green man on the moon argument."

Suppose for a minute that two scientists, Jack and Bill, are doing some scientific research for NASA. On one beautiful summer evening, Jack pulls out a telescope and takes a peek at the sky. He points his telescope towards the moon and shouts to Bill, "Bill, take a look! I see a green man eating toast on the moon!" Bill, being rather surprised, and a very mature and serious scientist, takes the telescope and peeks at the moon. He says, "Jack, I see nothing! Nothing. What little green man are you talking about? I see no man and no toast!" Jack takes the telescope away and takes another peek. And behold, there is the little green man eating toast on the moon! Jack responds, "Bill, I see the man. He's right there, eating toast." And once again

Bill takes the scope and sees nothing. By this time, Bill is irritated and tells Jack to prove it. Jack, on the other hand, is irritated that Bill does not believe him. What are they both to do? Well, being scientists, they resort to being inductive. But they cannot. You see, Jack sees the little green man, while Bill does not. Bill cannot prove *nor disprove* Jack's sightings. They are to be accepted *by faith*. Bill must assume that (1) Jack is lying, (2) Jack is hallucinating, or (3) Jack's little green man hides every time Bill takes a look.

Can you prove that the little man is or is not actually there? The truth is, if Jack truly sees the little green man, and if Bill does not, just because the green man hides every time Bill takes a peak, does not make the scenario *impossible*. Philosophers and scholars argue, for some strange reason, that if something cannot be disproven, it is meaningless. Well, my question is, if the little green man were an astronaut, and if the astronaut knew that when Bill looked to hide, what, then, do we do? Do we say that, because the astronaut's existence cannot be "disproved," he must not exist? Bologna! That is a ridiculous argument! We know that such a thing is possible. Thus, I argue that determinism is possible, even though it cannot be disproved. It cannot be disproved because it is beautifully accurate. It is so accurate that it cannot be disproved. However, if one can provide scenarios where there are reasonable flaws to the system—of which I am not aware of—the theory of determinism can be questioned. Until then, determinism, along with freewill (both, in my opinion, compatible) are fairly certain.

In conclusion, one's actions are reactions. However, in the end, the options do not become (a) or (b). The reactions only lead you to a multitude of choices. The determinism leads you to a number of choices—not just black or white. You choose from hundreds of things. Determinism only suggests that humans are limited in their actions because they were influenced by others' actions. Determinism (featuring freewill) teaches us that when you come to a fork in the road, it's not just left or right—its southeast, northeast, northwest, eastsouth, etc. We are predetermined to make decisions. We are predetermined to be limited. Predestination, from a determinists perspective, is merely an elimination—a narrowing down, so to speak—of choices. When I came to Barnes and Noble, it wasn't just Barnes and Noble versus the library. It was Barnes and Noble, Amazon, the library, my friend's house, my other friend's house, my friend's other library, etc. I had those choices available to me. That was *freewill*—the choice between all of the places I could have read books. Predestination (determinism) merely handed me the variety of choices, narrowed down from the rest of the 90 trillion choices available to humankind. In other words, others' peoples' actions merely help narrow down our choices. The fact that I was born in Russia, made my choices of cities to live in in the future, limited to Russian cities. Not that I was predestined to be in one certain city. And even in that city, I chose to live in some certain suburb. I could have chosen a different suburb. But I didn't.

It appears that our actions are, to some extent (and here there are some disagreements), in a very loose sense "predetermined." We cannot control everything. We cannot control our own impulses to such an extent that we override all of the things we have been predestined for—being born into a certain culture, religion, language and state, for example. We may not all call this "predestination," however, the things that move us in life other than our own will are truly there—they exist. There are things that motivate us that we are blind to. It appears that it is those who are "blind" that cannot fathom determinism. They simply aren't aware of exterior forces; forces that are exogenous. I believe that, no matter what our conclusions may be, predestined love is an absolute possibility. I will relate my own sentimental tales.

Once upon a time, I used to believe in Calvinism. I used to think that God controlled the world and that humans fulfilled the laws of God. Things went according to plan—the blueprint of God. However, my studies in sociology, science, religion, theology, and philosophy pointed me in a different direction. The evidence took me elsewhere. Thus, I am now very intolerant of Calvinism. (Ironically, I can almost sense the way Calvinists may use this paper as "proof" of their own beliefs.) I now see the world as a whole. I see God as someone who works all things for the good. He is simply fixing our mistakes—every once in a while. Those who are open to His Will and His Knowledge, partake in it and may find His ideas satisfying (which, I think, for the most part, are). Where has this left me? I have come to a conclusion that—along with determinism and freewill (both exactly compatible)—I embrace predestined love. A love that transcends time and space. A love that is absolutely divine. Something magical. I do not think, to be honest, that many have this sort of love—it is, after all, divine, and not many of us are holy and sacred. I firmly believe though, despite all of my critical thinking and doubt, that such a love exists. It is not bound by time because it is eternal. It's an energy that flows from God, the author and perfecter of love, to those around us. We are like gutters. We channel the love that comes from God to those around us. A gutter can contain lots of water, but it all comes from a source—and that source is the rain, coming from the heavenly clouds. God is our rain. It is an interesting concept.

My conclusion regarding predestined love is this: a soulmate can recognize his other half via the eyes. It's a love at first sight deal. You meet a person and something just clicks. You're like, "Wow, this is weird. I've never experienced this before." It's something that a ton of people are disillusioned by, too. Only time and experience prove us wrong. I have felt those "clicks" many times. Sometimes there would be fireworks. As time went on, I realized that my "connection" with someone else is more powerful. In other words, I progressively realized that we can "connect" with many varieties of people, but with some the connection is stronger than with others. It appears to me that I have found an answer: we have a variety of soulmates available to us; some, however, are better suited for us than others. If you were reading this on a Starbucks cup of coffee in four in the morning, it would read thus:

The Way I See It # 101: *If I were to meet a girl that enjoyed the same books I have enjoyed, listened to the same music I listened to, and shared a vast majority of other things with me, I would say one word: predestined. Why? Because, living in this cold world independent of each other, we have chosen similar paths. And this path that we are now on has been predetermined for us by someone or something else.*

It is relatively simple: people who live lives independent of each other but who chose similar things are doing something beyond their control. Imagine if two people, independent of each other, by listening to the same musicians, wrote a song that was virtually the same as the others'? Someone may call this chance. And I would say that such a conclusion is only fair—but I would not accept it. It's like saying that chance controlled where we were born. It wasn't chance. It was human action upon human reaction upon human reaction. Nothing, truly, happens independent of someone or something else—be it God or human. It seems to me that we are all intertwined and that our lives are voices in a symphony.

For example, I have not yet met a girl that I would call my soulmate. Why? Because in order for me to believe that she is my soulmate, I would require a number of things. First, she would have to, at the very least, enjoy my rants on love, relationships, God and philosophy. (Who could put up with such a venomous mixture?) Second, she would need to stimulate some sort of response from me that would be "beyond" my control; I would have to fall in love with her somewhat naturally, without knowing it. Third, we would both need to be madly in love with one another. Fourth, I expect a sort of connection to occur once we do meet. A love at first sight sort of experience. Why all of these things? Because predestined love is something that happens apart from one's complete will. It's like being born in Washington. It just happens. You're the child and you were born in a hospital in Washington. It just happens. Same with predestined love. All one can say in retrospect is, "It just happened!" As completely naïve and stupid and folly and imaginary and wonderful and fantastic as it all sounds, it is somewhat true. Because such a love rarely happens, I think it wise if most of my readers found my rant on this absolutely preposterous. (For such a love is almost contrary to nature, thus being miraculous, something David Hume would be strangely hateful of.)

Go ahead, say it. Say that I have lost my mind. And maybe I have, but at least I'm not the one stuck in a relationship that I am too afraid to love and too afraid to get out of. I'd rather be alone and satisfied (and cheerful) than stuck in a relationship that revolves around a woman's menstrual cycle and a man's bottle of Viagra. I think *such* relationships are, to be honest, fanatical and imaginary! They are based on nothing but negative thinking and the rejection of a view of love that embraces the magical.

It must be presupposed, already, even before one begins a discussion on love, that love is something magical. It is strange and weird indeed. It's something that we get a hold of and it is something that gets a hold of us (and we are too confused to figure out which it really is: whether it got a hold of us or weather we got a hold of it). I do not believe that love is something that must be defended. Socrates may have asked Meno what love was, instead of what virtue was, but that would have been beyond the point. Love is here and not-here; tangible and totally immaterial. Just like you cannot step into the same river twice (because the river changes constantly; once you step into it, the water is one thing, the next second, it is another), so it is with love. Every single time you fall in love, something ends up being changed. Yes, I readily admit that love has universal characteristics, but even those characteristics are so vague that it is hard to define love concretely. For example, the butterflies a girl feels in her stomach is directly related to love. However, you can get that on a rollercoaster (which love sometimes is!). One can say that they have crossed the same river a million times, only to fail to recognize that the river was different every time. How? The fish were in a different position. The water was of a different substance. The light was being reflected differently—once on a sunny day, the other time on a partly-cloudy day. The rocks were moved. The sand particles were constantly changing. That river that you thought you were so familiar with is really not so familiar! The river you thought you crossed a million times, really knew nothing of you—you were a complete stranger to it. So it is with love. Love can find you a million times and find you in a different place, in a different state of mind, every single time! Love is crazy!

Because of this, those of us who fall in love may only think we are in love. Just like the man who *thought* he crossed the same river twice. Which brings us back to the main concern: how do we know if we have been predestined for each other?

I do not know if a concrete answer is possible. It seems to me that, at least for some of us, we will be completely aware of the unique situation we are in when that moment comes. I have heard about many strange love stories. Many. I believe them. I know something greater is out there. We have been predetermined for something, but the responsibility is ours. Now that we are aware of our reactions, we must be aware of what we are reacting to. We must be aware of what it is we are doing. We must know what is influencing us. Once we are aware, we become enlightened and can do many great things. Thus, it seems to me that predestined love is something that creeps up on us, unexpectedly. We may be simply having a cup of tea at some regular coffee shop and there she might go. The most stunning girl in the world. Humming a song that you wrote and quoting a favorite quote that is tattooed on your sleeve. And then you just know it.

You really do. *Someday...*

CHAPTER TWENTY

The Contract: How Love Conquered Marriage

This rant is about The Contract of contracts. I deal here specifically with the institution of marriage and the consequences and implications of marriage. Personally, I think I am dealing with the question of marriage: why do we get married at all? As an aside, I inevitably deal with the question *par excellence*: what is love and why do we love?

Many young people today—in my warped opinion—would find the answer quite simple (or, at least, they assume it's simple): you fall in love and then you get married! Such an answer will find no friends amongst the letters contained in this writing. I believe that such a view of marriage is a very naïve and "teenage view" of marriage; it's a view held by a boy who just figured out that *orgasm* has nothing to do with biological *organisms*. It's the view held by the little girl who reads Cinderella. Surprisingly, the little boy and the little girl never grew up. The little folk that we are talking about may just as well be us. We all seem to believe that love just "happens": you meet a person of the opposite sex and immediately become attracted. Then. You. Get… Married!

Let's be real here, for a change: how many of us really believe such idiocy? Do teenagers really fall in love? And when these teens grow up, do they really love that significant other? And what is love anyways? And what is marriage?

The problem with marriage and love is that both are not understood by our oversexualized society. We tend to think of The Contract in terms of penis-meet-vagina; while love and marriage are to be understood in terms of reproduction and responsibility—something young little boys can never offer naïve little girls. Marriage is a contract between two people who will produce, promote and provide (for) a human being who will, eventually, become a part of a much larger society. Marriage is, essentially, at the root of the matter, really about sex. But not sex *per se*. (That's the naïve view.) Marriage is about a formation of a microcosm of society. It's about providing potential human beings for the continuance of human existence. If marriage was all about sex, we would simply have sexual relations with others; if marriage was all about reproduction, we would simply have sexual relations with as many people as possible (to increase our chances of our genetic survival); if marriage was all about love, we would not need the institution of marriage for something so abstract. Marriage, then, is something entirely different than mere sex and reproduction. Though that may sound like a contradiction, I will argue that it is not.

If humans merely wanted to reproduce, we would have simply had sex with as many partners as possible. We would try our best to promote ourselves into the future via our children. It seems, therefore, that reproduction does not necessarily require marriage, but marriage requires (potential) reproduction. But why do we reproduce?

One of the toughest questions for me to answer is the question of human existence and human reproduction (both closely related to each other). I cannot fake an answer here, however, I will attempt to answer the question. It seems to me that we reproduce for a number of reasons: (a) because we love sex; (b) because creating a human that is a cross between ourselves and the one we love is absolutely awesome; (c) because we want to have children to care for and love (and be loved and remembered in return); (d) because we want our genes to go into the future; and (e) because life requires this of us. All of these reasons, or some, are legit reasons for reproduction. But, still, why do we *need* to reproduce?

It seems to me that we reproduce because that is the ultimate purpose of life. If one were to take away reproduction from us—even the faint idea of it—many of us would not love sex so much. At least not me. What would sex be then? Just a couple of deluded people engaging in some weirdo horseplay with each other, who end up screaming, moaning and groaning in the end. Totally weird. Not cool. But toss the idea of potential reproduction in it and the picture becomes brighter (at least for me). The idea of "becoming one flesh" becomes more than just "real"—it *is* real. The idea of intimacy becomes exemplified via sex. Who thinks of unity and absolute intimacy when holding someone else's hand? Not many of us. Just because a body part touches another human's body part does not bring about feelings of absolute awe, unity and oneness. In fact, we touch other humans all the time with not a faint idea of absolute connection—I think that many such "encounters" are hardly memorable. But now throw sex in. What is sex without the idea of reproduction? You get a penis inside a vagina with some fluids. That's about it. You rock and roll for fifteen minutes and get a release of oxytocin and dopamine—which causes a "high." And then that's it. Unity? Does the idea of unity have to exist in "reproduction-less sex"? I argue no. What, then, is sex all about? Well, it is about reproduction. One may argue that many women do not want children and are willing to abort kids left and right (while using a ton of birth control pills per year). True, not all women want kids. But that does not annul my point. Such women are taught (brainwashed?) ahead of time into knowing and acknowledging that sex can lead to the production of a child. At least in theory, for such women, having sex can produce a literal "becoming [of] one flesh." But then you have the sterilized women who cannot get pregnant. Well, the idea of sex already carries with it such "intimate" ties and ideas that it, almost naturally, must induce some sort of unity, oneness, and intimacy. Thus, even the sterilized woman, who hates children and cannot get pregnant, engages in sex for obvious reasons: intimacy, intimacy, *orgasm*.

But what about the man? Why does he have sex? Me thinks for obvious reasons: intimacy, intimacy, orgasm. It's fun, it's fast, it's exciting, it's intimate, it's crazy; it has a short beginning, a short middle, and one heck of an ending! Basically, human beings long for sex because they want to reproduce. And those who don't want to reproduce engage in sexual activity because it brings a natural high and intimacy (oneness).

Ask yourselves this: would I have sex if there was no orgasm, no sensuality and no chance of reproduction? Who would have sex without the sensuality and the chance of making babies? Really? You would? You would stick a penis into a vagina and just move in and out for nothing? Why don't you just take a finger and pick her nose for her, that sounds more reasonable. All of that motion for nothing, imagine. I highly doubt that any one of us would have that sort of sex. Okay, I will be honest, maybe some of us weirdos would. But that doesn't mean that we would actually waste our time daydreaming about it. Moreover, not many of us would want to sign contracts to do *that*!

Nor would we risk getting STD's for that mundane crap! Imagine this conversation:

Brad: "Hey Jill, let's go have sex. You know, I'll stick it in, rock and roll, and do that for a couple minutes. You up for it?"

Jill: "Ummm...Last time it seemed sorta pointless, Brad. Besides, I don't want to get those nasty genital warts. I think I'll pass."

Brad: "Sounds good. I guess last night was pretty boring and meaningless."

Let's be honest here. Who would want such meaningless crap. Not many of us. Can I get an amen? Good.

If sex without reproduction is meaningless (without the idea of reproduction) then reproduction seems necessary. In fact, those who cannot stand their own creation must, at the very least, admit that the desire for sex is there for reasons of reproduction. Generally speaking, women are more interested in sex when they are ovulating. Which proves my point. If reproduction is as important as I think (genetically, emotionally, and mentally) then sex must go hand-in-hand with marriage. And if it be admitted that sex goes hand-in-hand with marriage, then marriage is, to an extent, about sex (and reproduction).

If marriage is about reproduction, then we have surely come full circle. Marriage is about having sex and reproducing. The keyword here is *reproduction*. To reproduce is not the same as to have sex (I'm saying this for the teenagers). Reproduction requires sex, but sex does not require reproduction. Just because you have sex does not mean that you will reproduce. But if you reproduce, it does mean that you have had sex. If sex is different than reproduction, then sex is not enough for reproduction. And if reproduction is the point of marriage (or, at the very least, an important point) then marriage must include not mere sex, but reproduction. But what is *reproduction*?

Reproduction is the ability of a certain species to produce duplicates of itself. A duplicate of a grown human being is not necessarily a newborn child, but a grown human being. Reproduction is the production of someone like yourself. In other words, if a species just produced newborns, and those newborns all died by age two, no one would say that the species is truly "reproducing." The species would, by all means, die out. To say the same thing, reproduction requires nurturing a "baby" to maturity. Reproduction requires nurturing, parenting, fathering, etc., etc. In other words, reproduction requires responsibility, love, reliability and commitment, amongst other things. A marriage, by inference, would require all that reproduction requires. If reproduction requires stability and commitment, then marriage requires stability and commitment; if reproduction requires sex, then marriage requires sex; if reproduction requires resources (monetary or organic) then so does marriage. Marriage requires all of that... and then some.

So why do we get married? Because we love sex. Because we love unity, intimacy and oneness. Because we have the "natural drive" to reproduce. But is marriage essential to society? Couldn't we do things differently? Of course we could. We could do things as Plato suggested in his *Republic*: we could have sex with certain people and have the city raise the children. We could have random sex and have the city raise the children. We could have random sex and just care for one another's children. In theory, we could do many things.

But would those things bring goodness, satisfaction, happiness and practicality? Would it be practical for you to have sex with someone who doesn't care for you? Would it be practical to have a mother raise the neighbors kids while neglecting her own? In theory we could do many things. We could, for example, not breathe but have machines do that for us. We could all wear oxygen tanks and be intubated. We could, for example, walk on our hands and not on our feet. We could.

Would mother's want others raising their children? Just ask any mother who cares for her child, who is a replica of her. But maybe we were all brought up to think that such a social system is abnormal. Maybe.

Is marriage essential to society? I think it is. But why? Because, in my opinion, marriage—traditional marriage—is a grand idea. What do I mean by "marriage"? I merely mean the idea where two heterosexual people live together, have sex, love one another, share a friendship and work together. Two people who are agreeing to live by a standard. Who are sworn in. Who have signed The Contract. But does marriage require all of those things? Do people have to sign contracts? Well, doesn't reproduction require long-term commitment? (Do not confuse sex with reproduction!) Doesn't marriage require commitment? A commitment to raise children—*your* (freakin') children. I think that marriage does require a political contract. Marriage is an act of politics—to promote the propagation of the human species. Does that, then, mean that I see marriage as merely reproduction? No. I see marriage as a commitment to reproduce while maintaining friendship and love. Why would I want to mate with someone I don't love? Marriage doesn't require that. I could reproduce with people that I don't love outside of marriage. Marriage, then, is much more than just reproduction. However, as I have pointed out earlier, reproduction is the point of marriage—naturally, reproduction would feature itself many times in a discussion about marriage! If reproduction was not the point of marriage—if, for example, the point of marriage was to just have sex and friendship—one would not need to have a contract, nor the notion of marriage. One would just need a casual friendship. Even if the relationship was long-term, then marriage is still not required. One could simply call it a sexual friendship, or something along those lines—but *not* marriage. A sexual friendship presupposes sex, *not* reproduction. Reproduction presupposes marriage, which presupposes commitment, which presupposes some sort of *contract*.

But why commitment? Why should we reproduce and watch our children? Why can't we be like the Romans and leave the children "exposed" by the hills? Let them die. Who cares for children! Well, if such is the case, we would merely need to have sex then. Why would we be, as a peoples and a society, interested in marriage? We would not even have come up with such a "ridiculous" idea. If life is merely about pleasing ourselves, then unrestrained, uncommitted sex is a perfect idea in such a world. We would not want children. We would spend our days having sex and seeking pleasure. All sorts of pleasure. Eventually, in a few years (50 years or so), all of the females would be 50 years of age or older—too old to reproduce. We would die out and that would be the end of it. I, honestly, see no point in such a life. But maybe Hugh Hefner does.

What should The Contract contain? I think that The Contract should contain a few important points. Reproduction should be mentioned, along with commitment, friendship, love, honesty and respect. Such things are a novelty in today's (and yesterday's) world. The Contract should be signed by those who are willing to share equal political powers, equal decision-making powers, responsibility, friendship, mutual agreement, and commitment. Commitment is extremely important.

For reproduction does not, sadly, presuppose love. But it does presuppose commitment, which, philosophically, makes commitment somewhat grander and more valuable in marital terms. When a couple has children, it is its duty—at least in theory—to raise children. The children born are dependent upon the parents. If the love "passes," commitment must excel. The children should not be left. A commitment is, after all, a commitment. It presupposes troubles—again, in theory. If the couple faces some sort of dilemma, The Contract cares not for the dilemma. Sure, the language may sound harsh, but think about material things. Look at your housing contract. If you even think about forgetting to pay the bill, you are kicked out on the street. No one cares about your troubles at home. Nobody cares about your abusive husband. (If he is abusive, I would promote, at the very least, counseling [for him] and separation [for you and the children].) Nobody cares about any of those things. You agreed to pay such-and-such a price in spite of the potential risks involved. The same goes for The Contract. If things don't work out, The Contract cares less about your personal satisfaction; it cares more about your children, the very future, than it cares for you. The Contract doesn't want you to make a stupid decision, nor does The Contract wish that you end up being "screwed." It is in the best interests of The Contract for a couple to reproduce, have a great sex life, and have an amazing atmosphere for the children (which The Contract protects). If the couple screws up,

The Contract is not to blame—it is merely a mediator of a greater message: the message that sex, reproduction, family, friendship and love are serious matters. Very serious matters. The Contract merely reminds each human of the seriousness of the situation. It acts as a law—it creates civil obedience. In fact, The Contract *is* a law.

Imagine a society where reproduction is not controlled. Imagine a society where law is nonexistent. Imagine a society that has no Contract. A society where one is not reminded of the seriousness of family life nor is bound by any law. What would such a society look like? It would be a society full of passionate idiots. Human beings have presupposed the goodness of laws. We have presupposed our corrupt and selfish nature. In fact, civil law presupposes humanity's depraved nature. Had humans "naturally" been good, laws would not exist. But because humans commit crimes and do harm to one another (consciously), we have laws. We have laws and contracts. But why contracts? Because we know people like to lie. They like to be irresponsible. And contracts are not merely papers. They have power. The power to bind and the power to loose. A contract makes sure that *you* do whatever it is that you have committed yourself to doing. And if you don't do it, there is a punishment involved. Laws and contracts presuppose crime and punishment. Laws and contracts maintain their worth and exercise their power via threats. What would our law look like if there was no punishment if you broke that law? Would the law be valued and respected? No! The same goes with a contract. It maintains power because of its ability to punish. The Contract is the same. It can punish you. In fact, it baffles me that no punishment follows a divorce. Something must be done about that. (At least, in such a world, punishment would follow.)

But who would want to sign such a contract? Ask yourself this: who wants to buy a house with a "credit card"? Well, it doesn't matter what your answer is, many do. And that is a matter of fact. No matter the consequences. If our materialistic society can punish us with hundreds of thousands of dollars regarding something as meaningless as a house, why must marriage, a spiritual, potentially eternal institution be treated with less seriousness? If marriage is the very thing that *makes* society—or, at the very least, the thing that *helps* create society—then it should be rightfully protected by contract and by law; a contract, if broken, punishable under law.

What are laws? Why do we have them? In theory, laws exist because people need to be told what to do. That is the simple, short answer. No buts, no ifs, and no whats. In fact, the simple answer is actually the most truest. Look at it this way: laws exist to tell people what to do. For example, people need to be told to buckle up and wear seatbelts when driving a vehicle. Why? Couldn't humans figure that out on their own apart from some sort of law? Well, yes, but humans have the irritating ability and bad habit of breaking laws. Every once in a while. So you have the mother who is driving to work one day, she's speeding because she is late. She isn't buckled up. She is putting on makeup. She is talking on her cell phone with her son. She is texting on her daughter's phone with her husband. And she is looking up the driving directions to the nearest Starbuck's on her navigation system. This is the sort of thing good, rational, and "law-abiding" citizens are capable of. How many of you are guilty likewise? Be honest. The point is this: we are capable of breaking even the most lax and "pointless" laws. The problem, however, is also this: the mother that was doing all of those things—namely, putting on makeup, not wearing a seatbelt, sexting while driving—was pulled over by a police officer. He stopped her and gave her a ticket of over five hundred dollars (laws require punishment upon being broken). He also reminded her kindly that such driving was relatively "reckless." He cautioned her to drive safely and not to be distracted. What the woman did not know was that she was about to kill a family of five had the officer not stopped her. She would have been guilty of murder. Murder? Just for texting while driving and being distracted? Yes, murder. Hadn't she willingly done all of those things? Didn't she know that such behavior can lead to such an outcome? She had to have known. The officer, in other words, saved her from committing a crime. A severe crime. But what exactly was the officer doing? He was, in short, a mediator of the law. He acted between the state that enforced the law and the human who was capable of following the law. He punished the woman, who agreed to the terms of the "societal contract," because she, though knowing her actions as being illegal, continued to pursue them. This is the way "societal contracts" work. We get punished for breaking laws.

Nonetheless, the question still remains: why do we have laws? As the previous story suggests, people need to be constantly "reminded" regarding the seriousness of certain actions. They need to be reminded how to conduct themselves properly. People need to be told what to do, in other words. Another example will suffice. Many of us go to the doctor when we become sick. We submit to his "authority" because we know that we aren't smarter than him. We ask a "specialist" to tell us what to do, how to live, and what foods to eat. We don't think there's anything wrong in a doctor telling someone not to eat McDonald's. In fact, we probably wish, deep inside, that every fast-food restaurant closed for good (for the overall benefit of society). We find such suggestions from authorities as "okay" and normal. We don't call doctors selfish dictators. Likewise with society. Political philosophers need to figure out what benefits society as a whole. They figure out what is most useful and they implement it. To look at the seatbelt example again, many people die each year in motor vehicle accidents because they are not wearing seatbelts. On the other hand, a small minority of people are probably harmed by the seatbelt. Thus, the political philosopher must create a law that would serve the majority of the population. In other words, *laws will not benefit everyone*. If McDonald's, for example, were to be closed down—had a law been passed to shut down unhealthy food chains—McDonald's would suffer from such a law. But the majority of people, if they begin eating healthy, would benefit from such a law. Thus, every law does have its limitations; I openly acknowledge that.

So why do we go to see the physician? Because we do not know everything. We are not walking and talking encyclopedias (though I may be!). We are, then, flawed creatures. We have holes in our logic and in our thinking (just like doctors). We do not know the reasons for some of our actions nor do we know the outcomes. We have a knowledge deficit. This "knowledge deficit" serves as an important factor in making it probable that we will commit the crime of doing something "wrong." We may, for example, eat some sort of fruit or mushroom that is poisonous to our bodies. Though such an action was intended for the benefit of our body (i.e., we originally intended to nourish our body) it turned out to be rather harmful (and potentially, in some cases, fatal). Humans, in other words, make mistakes (which can be empirically demonstrated). Such mistakes make us susceptible to being guilty of breaking societal law. Because a person can make the choice of texting and driving (and potentially killing someone, which has, of recent times, happened one time too many), a person needs law. We need laws because we make mistakes. We need laws because our nature is, to some extent, corrupt. Laws would not exist had people been perfect and had they done things that were of absolute benefit to themselves and to society as a whole. The law not to murder, for example, is a reminder for those of us who wish to murder that such a thing, according to the law, is not beneficial to society. This is not the place for me to talk about justice and law more in-depth; it is merely my intention to show humans that laws are beneficial.

Returning to the original argument: what has marriage, love, society and law to do with one another? As my previous discussion has shown, we get married because we have a natural drive to reproduce. (This is something that we cannot control. The desire to have sex and reproduce dominates many a thought.) We get married because we want to not merely have sex, but we want to (need to?) reproduce. I have adamantly pointed out the difference between sex and reproduction. I want to point it out again. To have sex, one need not reproduce; to reproduce, one needs to have sex, generally speaking, and desires this much so. At the end of the marriage cycle, all that will remain are children. To reproduce precludes responsibility and stability. A mother and father (hopefully together) will raise their children to a suitable age (18 or 21). This "age of maturity" concludes the cycle of reproduction. To reproduce means to bring forth, into the future, a replica of your species. That "replica" is not merely a child, but, according to my definition of reproduction, a mature adult. Thus, to reproduce means to bring one's children to maturity. As I have previously pointed out, a population is technically not reproducing if all of the "replicas" (i.e., children) die young. Such a species becomes extinct. Reproduction entails more than just producing children; it entails raising them to a stage of maturity. To do that, at least for *homo sapiens*, that requires 18-21 years (21 years, in my personal opinion). Thus, to bring this full circle, if marriage has reproduction as *one* of its *many* cornerstones, then marriage includes and *presupposes a long-term heterosexual relationship lasting at least eighteen years*. That is a powerful statement. By my definition, and those who want to disagree are more than free to do so, marriage includes the following "cornerstones":

(a) Reproduction. This involves a long-term relationship, responsibility and commitment—a commitment that far exceeds the illusionary and fleeting feelings of modern love.

(b) Sex. This act is presupposed in the first statement, since, generally speaking, humans do not become pregnant unless they engage in sex. (Excluding Mary, the Mother of Jesus Christ.) Sex also creates a "pull" and a "desire" for the opposite sex, which is natural and inescapable. This desire for sex helps form a heterosexual relationship and helps create unity—the two shall become one flesh.

(c) Love. Whatever one thinks of love, and however one defines it, love is essential for the proper raising of children. Though reproduction can, in theory, progress without love, such children will probably not be as healthy emotionally as those raised in a loving family.

(d) Relationship. A relationship is, to be blunt, the most important thing in marriage. One would not have it had there not been a relationship in the first place! Thus, everything that I have been dealing with, in fact, presupposes relationships. And, to take this even further, relationships presuppose the idea that humans are *social creatures*.

(e) Society. A marriage is a society in itself. Marriages occur between, at least, two different humans. These humans have been brought up by two different families (usually). The will and desire to become married is already a social act—therefore, society is an important part of marriage. Marriages create society, literally.

To summarize, as briefly as possible, all that I have said thus far, it seems to me best to take all of this information and project it into a real-life scenario. Thus, I will try to recapitulate everything in a short story and discuss the philosophical implications, whenever the need arises, in a "Platonic dialogue" manner.

The Contract of Marriage: A Short Example

Luke meets Tully and they both fall in love (I will discuss love later on in the paper). For whatever reasons, they decide to get married. Luke loves Tully and feels "whole" whenever she is around. He finds himself thinking about her constantly. He has never felt like this about anyone and feels as if this love is something divine and supernatural. Tully, too, feels madly in love with Luke. She loves the way he cares for her and she loves sharing long nights with him, together. She admires his ability to understand her and loves his company. They are, to be sure, good friends and lovers. Tully is preparing for the wedding day and is busy making plans. Luke is busy finding odd jobs to help pay for everything.

There arises a first question: why are Luke and Tully getting married? It seems that they are getting married because that's what people who are in love do. But why marriage? Why not something else? Why not just live together? Why have a social occasion, such as a marriage feast? Why obtain a marriage license? What is all the fuss about? It appears that we are asking ourselves a timely question: why marriage? Before we can consider an answer, we must look into the *motives* behind marriage. Everybody has a motive. We do things for a *reason*. We get married for a reason. So the question should be: what is the reason for Tully marrying Luke?

There are, to be sure, many reasons why Luke and Tully are getting married. Firstly, both are in love with one another. They are in love and have formed a bond together. They are social creatures, which is presupposed, who have engaged in social conduct and have found each other to be socially compatible and friendly. They are, in other words, not lonely—no longer in isolated prison, to use an analogy. Not only are they socially suitable for one another, they are also attracted to one another. But why are they attracted physically to one another? Couldn't Luke have gone for the brunette next door? The answer is not so simple here. Attraction is one of the few things that we are, literally, "born with." You can't help yourself with attraction. You do not just become attracted. Some of us love brunettes. Why? Well, we don't know, we just do. Some of us think someone is pretty, but we don't find them attractive and appealing in a more deeper sense. For example, I find many women beautiful. But I don't find them attractive (where they "attract" me to them). There is something that attracts us to select individuals, this *something* is more than just our mind; it is beyond our conscious control. (Though it could be subconscious, but that would be another argument.) In other words, Luke found Tully attractive for reasons he probably couldn't tell you. Once he found her attractive, he, naturally, being "attracted," walked towards her. He may have engaged in some petty talk about the weather, or the like. Later on, he may have tested her waters. He would have examined what she was made of. Did she share similar interests? Did she love the same philosophers? Did she cook foods he liked? Was it socially possible for the two to be friendly—to meet the social void we all have? (This writing presupposes that all humans are social creatures.) Once he found her interesting, and once he could spend his social time with her, their mutual attractiveness led to friendship; their friendship would have led to time spent alone; their constant mingling would have led to a progressive social bond—a bond that goes deeper than many sociologists and psychologists wish to acknowledge. They would have become so intermingled with one another, that one couldn't dream of being apart from the other—this "social fusion" would be what the ancients called soulmates. Where two separate and individual souls choose to, freely, become one with each other. In other words, "soul fusion" has occurred.

But, still, why are they getting married? As it so happens, friendship, social bonding, relationships end up leading to what may be called "love." Erotic-love, to differentiate it from other social forms of love, is a sexual love (at least in my writings). This erotic, sexual-love, is what really lies at the root of erotic-love. A friendship between a man and a woman can include everything—social bonding, friendship, relationship, love—but once it includes sexual desire, we are dealing with erotic-love—love that goes beyond love. Love that seeks some sort of sexual and sensual pleasure. Love that is more intimate. Surely having sex with someone is more intimate than having a thousand dinners. (At least the sort of sex that I am imagining. But you wouldn't know.) This erotic-love, then, by nature, is seeking intimacy. In other words, at this stage in the social relationship, the man and woman are not mere friends, they are potential marriage material. They don't just want to have candle light dinner together, they want to feel the throbs of hot sex. They want to mate. And not just mate and have sex (for that is merely sensual), they want to *reproduce*. And the moment one throws in reproduction, as I have defined it—remember, eighteen or more years!—that is the moment the idea of marriage is born. (I will define love more in-depth later on in this paper. This will suffice for now.)

The idea of marriage is to be seen on a historical continuum. Marriage doesn't just "happen." You cannot say that marriage just occurred. It is not a single act (or action). Marriage, I repeat, is not to be defined as a *single act*. Marriage is a process. It is as historical as Independence Day; you can trace its development, its creation, formation and continuation. Marriage progressively continues. *Homo sapiens* are never "married"; they are in the *process of marriage*. If marriage is, by (my) definition, a reproductive institution, it presupposes everything that reproduction entails. And reproduction requires time, energy, love, money, commitment, health, responsibility, etc., etc. It requires a plethora of things.

Marriage is as natural as sex. It is occurring around us because it is beneficial to the progression of our society (I do know that some would find this statement problematic). Luke and Tully are getting married because they have chosen to—whether by will or genetic inclination—to have not just mere sex (for to have casual sex, one does *not* need to get married—please keep that in mind throughout my discussion) but to *reproduce*. I am not trying to make marriage sound as if it is all about sex—that would be a misinterpretation of my message. I am, however, saying that what sets marriage apart from casual sex, and other forms of relationships, is responsibility, long-term commitment and reproduction. These go hand-in-hand with marriage. Luke and Tully have decided to reproduce. Had they decided to have sex, they could have had sex. So what. They could have had sex a million times. Again, so what. That *doesn't* require marriage. In today's unrestrained society, people have sex outside of marriage all the time. Therefore, sex with someone else does not qualify one for marriage. (An argument I will later elaborate on against the institution of homosexual *marriages*.) Since sex is not what distinguishes between friendships and even erotically passionate friendships (where sex is also included), *reproduction* is what I hold to be a true distinction (though not without its own problems). It is essentially the desire to reproduce that brings Tully and Luke to their wedding day. It is that desire that is so powerful, natural and inescapable.

One may object by saying that infertile couples get married. True, infertile couples get "married." They are, however, getting married after the fact. The fact that what originally constituted marriage (i.e., reproduction) is eliminated in an "infertile" marriage only implies that terms are being bent. Let me provide an illustration. In today's society, many people have sex. Traditionally, sex meant vaginal penetration by a male penis. (Though such a definition does not apply to all societies—but that means nothing to my argument.) In America, sex was understood to be between a male and a female, vaginal penetration included. Despite this fact, many have had "sex" not in the so-called "traditional" manner: teenagers are trying things like oral sex, anal sex, and in-between-the-thighs sex, amongst other forms of "sex." The term is being loosely applied to any form of "sexual" pleasure. If it be proven that traditionally sex meant sex when a vagina was penetrated by a penis, then it must be admitted that all of these "recent" modifications must be called something else. Likewise with marriage. Just because marriage originally meant a coming together of two (or more) heterosexual humans for purposes of reproduction, does not mean that a person who meets all other criteria (i.e., friendship, love, commitment) should automatically and consciously change the term "marriage" to something else, like "erotic-sexual, long-term friendship." One may object by saying that homosexual lovers can then also contract marriages (for they cannot reproduce, but they meet the "other criteria" I have mentioned). The problem with this is that an infertile couple, especially in the ancient days, did not know beforehand who was or was not infertile. The presupposition in marriage was *reproduction*. However, it is to be acknowledged that marriages that included infertility were to be expected. People knew that risks were always involved. Thus, a marriage could still be conducted between a man and a woman and be considered a marriage even after the couple (later on) found out that one or the other (or both) were infertile. In fact, to make my point, in the ancient days, a man could divorce his wife simply on the grounds of infertility. Why? Because marriage presupposed reproduction. If one was "married" and had no children, why be married? A marriage, as I have adamantly pointed out, served (and continues to serve) as an institution where reproduction is a cornerstone, if not *the* cornerstone. A "marriage," then, between a man and a man, or a woman and a woman, is, in theory, impossible. If the purpose is reproduction, for the continuation of society (marriage is very much a political and social institution), then a marriage between two homosexuals (or however many) defeats the purpose. In fact, it defies the very term. (Though many try to "update" the term "marriage" and make it apply to a million things, which, to me, sounds ridiculous.)

Rants on Love

Okay, so let us focus our attention back to Luke and Tully again. What motivates Luke to marry Tully? We have already decided that humans are (a) social creatures; (b) in need of loving relationships with one another; and (c) engage in sex for pleasure and reproduction (within marriage). Since these few basic things underlie marriage, why, in fact, are Luke and Tully going through with all of this? Sure, sex sounds great (but you can do that outside of marriage); good friendship sounds fine too (again, you can have great friendships outside of marriage); and reproduction sounds good—within long-term marriage, but why get married *and reproduce* in the first place? If Luke and Tully have sexual desires towards one another, why not "tie the tubes" and have endless sex (without any "consequences")? Why not just have a long-term relationship (cohabitation) and have lots of sex, intimacy, love, romance, etc. without any babies? The answer is two-fold: (1) many women, speaking from personal experience here, want to have children—it's like a "natural" thing for them (I can care less what lesbian feminists think of this statement—the burden of proof lies with the select few "heretics" who think otherwise); and (2) reproduction happens because of our desire to continue society—after all, without sex *and reproduction* (until maturity and beyond), society ceases to exist (if the lesbian feminists don't believe me, they should try it). Thus, it seems to me that humans reproduce for a number of easily identifiable and verifiable reasons. Human beings, being social creatures, crawl out of their dark mammoth caves and seek thee light. They meet another human being and feel delighted. It is this social delight that marks the root and seed of society—in taking that first step towards social fellowship, human beings began what we now call a "society." Thus, to take us back to the theory of origins, it seems as though society was born when two human beings began interacting with one another. Eventually, that interaction—albeit a very heterosexual one—led to the formation of society's microcosm: the family unit. A child was born. This *social* (I am purposefully overusing the term here) interaction was instigated by humanity's need for man-to-man fellowship. Even today, one of the worst punishments a human being can experience is incarceration in an "isolation room." The most damaging thing a human can experience is separation from other human beings. This "social gene" is presupposed in all of my writings.

The question still remains: why get married? It appears that reproduction is at the core of marriage. As I have earlier somewhat briefly argued, sex without reproduction is phenomenon-less—it is, at least in my opinion, devoid of any real meaning. As I have stated, sex that doesn't presuppose reproduction—a literal becoming of two in one flesh—is a meaningless and dry form of sex. It is my opinion that the very idea of sex carries with it connotations of unity. Thus, even when homosexuals today have anal "sex" they are engaging in an activity that has been wired in the human genome to represent "unification." Which is why "reproduction-less sex" still can be, in theory, "meaningful." Because it still carries with it the ancient notion and awe of reproduction. Thus, couples who are engaging in sex that shares nothing with reproduction can still, somewhat deviously, have the original meaning and awe of sex be projected into the reproduction-less sex act itself. In fact, I think the word "projection" sums up my view nicely. Also, it is inconceivable that humans would want to have sex had reproduction and pleasure been impossible, which further helps demonstrate that the value of sex is based upon two things: (a) sexual gratification and (b) reproduction. When one, in theory, eliminates reproduction, one, somewhat arbitrarily, destroys much of what sex is all about.

Thus, summing this part up, it appears that reproduction (sex) is at the very heart of marriage. But why? If one were to eliminate sexual gratification, would humans still "reproduce" and commit the sexual act? I will argue yes. Why? Because, sexual gratification or no, humans will have the desire to reproduce. Sex, then, in my view, rests on the *cornerstone of reproduction*—sexual gratification, though contained in the sex act, is *not on par* with reproduction. This idea further demolishes the idea that "sexual acts" between homosexuals are truly meaningful—take away the societal projection of unity, reproduction and intimacy unto sex and the homosexual "sex act" becomes nothing but a sham act of mere sensual gratification. If sex—along with inevitable reproduction—is so important, why do human beings have the desire to get married and reproduce? As I posited earlier, even if sexual gratification were to be taken away from the sex act, humans would still, in my opinion, reproduce. This is where the question comes full circle—why do humans want to reproduce?

Everyone knows that humans get married to reproduce (most of us) and that humans, naturally, following genetic instinct, desire to have sex. Sex, as in sexual gratification, can easily be explained away: everyone wants to feel a release of oxytocin and dopamine. People love sex. Yes, but why do people love reproduction? People get artificially inseminated for non-sexual—even asexual—reasons. The question is why. I believe that people reproduce for a number of reasons:

(a) People reproduce because they want their existence to be "immortalized" in their children and their childrens' children. In other words, people want their children to carry their personal legend—dreams and ambitions—into the limitless future. To say the same thing in different words, people want to be famous. If only for a day.

(b) People reproduce because they have a natural desire for sex, which, inevitably, leads to potential reproduction (unwanted pregnancies?).

(c) People reproduce because they want to "love" someone. (I have "empirical evidence" for this after working at a health clinic that saw young teen mothers. Many teens simply wanted to be pregnant to love someone and to be loved. No buts about that.)

(d) People reproduce because their love for their spouse is "realized" in a child. My daughter will remind me not only of myself, but of my wife. In loving my wife and myself, I will, too, love my daughter. It is, to be sure, somewhat related to (c)—however, the love I have for my wife is "extended" to my daughter via my wife.

(e) People reproduce because they have a natural desire not only for sex, but for *reproduction*. Nature wants and needs to continue into the future.

(f) People reproduce because it is their way of saying "thank you" to the previous generation who has given "birth" to the couple itself. In reproducing, the couple is giving back what was freely given it; namely, a chance to be human. A chance to love and be loved. The gift of life is marvelous indeed! It is to be freely given (to your own children—*future*) and freely received (from your parents—*past*).

Although there may be more reasons for human reproduction, these shall suffice for this discussion.

It seems to me, then, that humans reproduce for societal reasons. We have already noted how humans crave social relationships. This social longing in humanity makes us want fellowship and, therefore, society. We actually long for society. It takes a man a few minutes with a group of females to recognize this need—which is most evident in the ovary-bearing human species. Humans love to socialize. This much is fact. Dogmatic fact. On top of that, humans, generally speaking, give back to society what they have taken from it (human life; babies, in other words). The need for fellowship and relationships seems to be a most certain driving force in human nature. It is an invisible force made visible through the sexual act. Humans seek fellowship and, thus, hope to find that most intimate fellowship in the sexual act. And heterosexual sex is all about society: it is about relationships and intimacy. Heterosexual sex contains within it the very secrets of society: intimacy, commitment, romance, friendship, unity, oneness, etc. It is, for example, well-known, at least to me, that in order for a man to bring a woman to orgasm, the man must, at first, create the most perfect, relaxing and soothing atmosphere. The duties of the woman must be numbed and forgotten. It's why women tend to reach orgasm sooner when on vacation—their mind is not tainted by everyday life. However, it is to be noted that, in order for the man to create such an atmosphere, a relationship is presupposed. Thus, the female sex, which is harder to please (correct me, ladies, if I am wrong), stimulates a man to develop a friendship with the woman before initiating sex. Sex, then, is a highly social activity. For the woman to be superbly pleased, the man must build that relationship and that atmosphere which leads up to sex and female orgasm. I think that the female species was thus purposefully *designed*—God wanted men to be more social and human, so He gave us women. Why women? They drive us crazy and we must begin sex in the kitchen in the early morning. The desire for sex and the need to please and pleasure one's wife brings a man to a point of decision: for those things to exist simultaneously, a man must work to create a soothing atmosphere for his wife. This "soothing atmosphere" is, then, a *work* of art. (Emphasis on the work.) The man must strive to please his wife. As early as the early morning. (No, making a pot of coffee in the morning doesn't count!) In doing so, the man, whether he is aware of it or not, is building a relationship with the woman. This, then, results in the social bond between a husband and wife—the fusion of two souls. All in all, in my opinion, sex is an act of unity. It is an act of friendship. It is an act of reproduction, which is intimately related to oneness.

Luke and Tully, then, are getting married for reasons unbeknownst to them. They are motivated by a multitude of factors. Most of these factors, however, are directly related, in some way, to relationship, fellowship, society, friendship and intimacy. (All of these things are virtually synonymous with one another.) Marriage constitutes the roots of society. Marriage is the very institution that bears the grunt of society. But what form of marriage is to be preferred for the benefit of society? "[M]onogomous unions—one man married to one woman—predominate because it is the most efficient marital form. Polygamy is encouraged when the sex ratio is significantly different from unity and when men or women differ greatly in wealth, ability, or other attributes." It seems that monogamy is to be preferred (one man and one woman). However, economically speaking, if the ratio between the male species and the female species is out of balance, polygamy *may* be an acceptable form of marriage.

Throughout this brief and very eccentric discussion, I have focused my attention on marriage and its relationship to sex, reproduction and intimacy (i.e., relationships, friendship, fellowship, unity, oneness, etc.). I have argued that marriage has everything to do with reproduction, and that reproduction itself has to do with human social interaction (the need for intimacy and fellowship). All in all, everything goes back to social interaction. Humans are social creatures. Everything we breathe has to do with society. Because society is so important to us, and because we would not exist apart from heterosexual sex acts and reproduction (nourished by responsibility and commitment featured in marriage), we, humans, stick together. We cherish each others' existence and genuinely seek companionship with each other. This companionship reaches its greatest form in heterosexual sex and completes itself in the sex act that results in reproduction (i.e., the birth of a child). The birth of a child ensures that the child will help propagate society. However, that is done only if other heterosexual couples are also reproducing. Thus, the child ends up growing up amongst his own kind (being socially active). This reproductive cycle gives children and adults the ability to maintain social connections.

Reproduction serves, to be sure, a more essential function also. The law of the universe is based on entropy: things are always moving towards destruction without energy input. You leave a house standing for a hundred years, untouched, and it will fall to the ground. What once was a beautifully decorated mansion will be nothing but a useless pile of dust and ashes. Don't use your muscles for a while and they, too, will atrophy. (Which is why nurses and doctors continuously stress weight-bearing activity.) The human body, empirically speaking, tends to grow old with age—inevitably—and goes from a state of health to a diseased state. This destruction is attributed to apoptosis—programmed cell death. Namely, our human body, though having continuous input of energy sources (food, movement, chemical reactions, etc.), regardless moves towards destruction. In defiance of the second law of thermodynamics—which states that in all energy exchanges, if no energy enters or leaves the system, the potential energy of the state will always be less than that of the initial state. Defying this law, our cells, in clear defiance of modern evolutionary thought, turn against themselves and, via apoptosis, are programmed to die (kill themselves, commit suicide, etc.). Even though an old man continues to eat (put energy into his human system), his body, contrary to the second law of thermodynamics, is killing itself despite the energy inputs. In theory, if the modern premises of evolution were correct—namely, that living organisms move from less complex to more complex systems, while consistently choosing "life" over death—then the old ninety-year-old man should, in theory, continue to live. For, according to the second law of thermodynamics, energy input decreases entropy (disorder) and creates, to some extent, "life." However, the old man eats and continues to progressively grow more and more "sick." Why? Apoptosis. Programmed cell death. Evolutionary thought is wrong in the sense that life does not necessarily create life, it seems, on the contrary, that the human body (and all other living systems) move towards not life but *death*. Instead of human beings evolving, as is supposed, into more complex, more developed, more adept creatures, human beings, are, in reality, already programmed to die from day one. Because humans die, and will continue to die (I suppose), we must produce children. Why? What do children have to do with human life? Because children take care (put energy into) their parents, and thus, allow life to continue. Human beings are absolutely *dependent* upon someone else for the first few *years* of life *and* are dependent the last few *years* of life. Human beings are, by all means, absolutely dependent for years on end throughout their lifespan. Adult parents take care of their little children and then the adult children take care of their dying and aging parents. This is the cycle of life. Dependency. (Forget everything you thought you knew about "independent" America.) In order for society to function properly, families need to have children. More than two children per every heterosexual couple. This inevitability is what lies beneath reproduction, society, relationships and marriage (love, too). If human beings have sex and reproduce *because* of their need and desire for society (remember, we are social creatures at our core), then human beings care for life and relationships. They care for life because life is what allows us to engage with one another. It is no wonder that old people want to live too! Just ask your aging grandma. In other words, life is presupposed for human interaction (relationships, fellowship, intimacy, sex, etc.). Thus, humans also have a drive and need to survive (as long as possible) in spite of apoptosis. (Our eternal souls play a different tune than our mortal bodies.)

All of this suggests that human beings seek life and social interaction with other human beings. These two things are presupposed in everything from marriage to sex to death. If every couple had one child, this would not benefit society. This would continuously decrease the population by cutting it directly in half with every generation. But, if I am correct (which I believe I am), if life is all about living and relationships, then human beings long not merely for each other, but for reproduction (which only continues and enhances life and social interaction). Thus, a society that does not reproduce is doing things contrary to nature. A society that has less than two children per couple is also working against itself. People in America and other countries will soon experience "shock by gray." Our generation enhanced birth control, abortion and promoted societal childlessness. The next few years will produce a wave of older people who have no one to take care of them (a complete societal disaster). This influx of "old people" (as if we couldn't predict this?) will prove devastating to our society. This imbalance of "energetic youth" with the "energy-dependent elderly" will cause absolute disarray and chaos. The energy needed to keep the elderly (energy-dependent) alive will not be produced by the limited youth. Energy can only go so far. Ten youth can only take care of so many people (and let me tell you, the numbers are not infinite—not even close). This entire argument can be summed up thus: heterosexual couples are essential to society and must continue to reproduce with more than two children per every heterosexual marriage. Though life will continue to take its toll, though earthquakes will continue to take lives, though famines will kill millions, people need to "make up" for this societal deficiency. Humans need to be aware of life's purpose: reproduction, relationship and life. This further brings us to the next pressing question: if people marry to reproduce and have a relationship, where does love fit in? Have we done away with love?

Defining Love

What is love? Can we define it adequately or will it forever remain elusive? I will propose a number of things in this paper, first, however, I want to look at potential definitions of love. I want to look at reasons and motives for love. Why we love? What is love? How do we love? What do we get out of it?, etc.

To begin, people use the term "love" for a variety of different things. One can say that he or she "loves" cars and then turn around and say the same thing about a significant other. Is "love" for the car the same as love for a significant other? I highly doubt it. My heart doesn't skip a beat when I see my car, does yours? I can say I love my dog. I can say I love my cake, and then happily eat it. Does that mean that when I say that I "love" my wife, I would "eat" her? Clearly the term love is being used to mean entirely different (and even opposite) things! Sometimes we eat things we "love," other times we don't (as with your mom).

As early in ancient history as the Greeks, people began to distinguish between different types of love. The Greeks had a few main names for love: *agape*, *eros* and *philia*. *Agape* meant some sort of "unconditional love," a love that was very pure—synonymous with God's love (later Christian literature); *eros* was a passionate and sensual-sexual love, generally—we get our word erotic from it; *philia* was a love for a brother or friend, used more generically for general love—we get our word philosophy from combining *philia* (love) with *sophia* (wisdom), thus getting "love of wisdom."

Today in America, we have love and liking. We either love someone or we "merely" like them. We could "love" our mom and "love" our wives; we could have sex with one and not the other. This makes English a strange language indeed. In this paper, I will be using the word "love" to mean, unless otherwise specified, "heterosexual love"—a love between a man and a woman. Moreover, I will argue that this heterosexual-married love has sex as its most distinguishing attribute (thus, it would be somewhat similar to the Greek *eros*). Moreover, the term "love" in this paper will not relate to "friendship love" *per se*, nor the love between humans and cats or dogs or moms or brothers, etc. Of course I am being somewhat arbitrary doing that; however, due to the abstract and differing ideas concerning love, I choose to be somewhat direct and concrete—which, to be honest, poses not a few problems, for which, I am sure, you will forgive me.

It is rather obvious that the difference in America between "love" and "liking" has to do, more or less, with "depth"—how *deep* is the liking. This depth is what leads to or inevitably becomes what we call love. Thus, it would seem, that liking a person comes first; while love comes second. You first "fall in like" (as one of my girlfriends once put it) and then you "fall in love." The distinction is a matter of depth. Other than the issues of depth, philosophers and thinkers throughout the centuries have come to see love in a number of different ways. Some think love has to do with union ("the two shall become one"); others think love has to do with robust concern; others think it has to do with valuing another human being; and others think love has to do with mere emotion. Before we examine each theory, it would be perfect for me to state here that I think love involves all of these things; thus, for me, I don't have to pick and choose which theory sounds better. I believe *all* of them have something to say or recommend about love. However, I will examine and develop a theory of my own that explains most everything in the most simple manner. Such a theory—a theory that explains all or most of the phenomena simply—is the theory most likely to be correct. I will now turn to love as *union*. This is the theory I most align myself with. I will spend some time developing this theory and I will engage with a few potential critiques of it. In the foregoing discussion, I hope that you, my beloved readers, will discover and examine your *own* reasons for love. Only in such a way will this *provocative* writing be worthwhile—only if it truly proves to be thought-provoking and engaging.

Unified Love: The Two Shall Become One

When humans first began making an exit from their mammoth caves, they had one motive: survival. They needed to leave the moist and dark shadows of their caves in order to hunt animals and grow crops. But why would humans *want* to live and survive? What were their *reasons* for doing so? I believe people wanted to eat in order so that they may live. But why would they want to live? Because they wanted to continue to exist. But why would they want to continue to exist? What exactly was the point of their existence? I think they wanted to live and move about precisely because they wanted to live to enjoy fellowship with one another. They wanted to live and breathe so that they could be with one another. They were absolutely devoted to the cause of society, right from the start. They wanted to be social. Engaging with one another was the very *purpose* of life. In other words, fellowship, friendship, companionship, unity, oneness, etc., these were all things that humans sought (being virtually synonymous with one another). So did humans live to be social, or were they social in order to live? This is a question of *which came first, the chicken or the egg?* I believe that both are true at once. Humans lived in order so that they may socialize (they lived in order so that they may see their children, have relationships, etc.) and they socialized (hunted together, traded together, etc.) in order so that they may live. Both can be true at once. Nonetheless, the thing at the center of the issue was always the *pursuit of life* and *social relationships*. Since life is presupposed for any human interaction, we will now eliminate it from our discussion. That leaves us with only one thing that all things go back to: *social relations* (i.e., friendship, companionship, relationships, unity, oneness, etc.). Thus, at the very core of all human existence lies—simply put—*friendship*. But what exactly is friendship?

Friendship involves, at the very least, two or more human beings. From a very basic view, a person who "knows" someone else by name is, in theory, not a "friend." Therefore, when two humans meet, and when simple introductions have been made, what causes a human being to continue the conversation (which may develop later into friendship) or abort it? To me, the answer seems relatively simple: a human being will stick around and enjoy a conversation with a "total stranger" if the stranger shares something that the other human being is, at the very least, interested in or familiar with. Thus, a chemist would naturally draw a chemist stranger towards himself. Both will have something familiar to talk about (atoms, electrolytes, chemicals, etc.) and maybe something not-so-familiar—this I call "interesting." Though one of the chemist's may not know what the other is talking about (i.e., he is not exactly familiar with the subject, since it is new) he may stick around because he is interested in it.

Thus, there are really two outcomes that can occur when two strangers meet: they introduce each other and move on (due to lack of mutual agreements, familiars, and interests) or they stick together because of *commonalities* that *bind* them (almost out of their own natural will). When nothing familiar or interesting or common is *shared* between two random, "stranger-humans," the humans will, naturally, seek someone of their own kind. I believe this to be relatively well-established and universal. Exceptions may occur, but that is not the norm. Thus, friendship is a matter of *sharing commonalities*. If I am not interested, whatsoever, in microbiology, what would keep me around microbiologists? If I am not interested in rock music, why would I be interested in sticking around with a girl who is obsessed with rock (with whom I share nothing else in common)? In fact, everything I've said thus far is so firmly established that it seems relatively pointless in trying to argue against this most popular way of friendship. Human beings are like birds of a feather who flock together. The ancient and most-wise Jesus ben Sira wrote, "Birds roost with their own kind…" (Sirach 27:9 NRSV). Clearly Jesus ben Sira experienced a very similar sense of friendship 2, 200 years ago. People who are alike gather together. In the New Testament, a similar idea is also found (2 Cor. 6:15). People today haven't changed much since Jesus' day: we still gather together because of commonalities.

It seems, then, that after two strangers meet, the first thing that happens is a sort of "bonding." The two (or more) random humans bond together via similar experiences and commonalities. The question is: do we become friends *because of* our similarities or do we have similarities because of our friendship? That is a good question. Correlation is not always causation. I think both answers are compatible. I may initially become "acquaintances" with a girl because we both admire Blaise Pascal. Later on, however, she may influence me to like Jesus and I may influence her to like Tertullian. In other words, our initial commonality was Pascal; however, as our unifying friendship developed, we both began to influence one another. Thus, the answer to the previous question is an adamant yes. We do become (initial) friends because of our similarities (at first); but then we move on to become deeper friends and remain friends because of our increase in mutual interests (her influencing me to like Jesus, me influencing her to read the writings of Tertullian). What, then, makes an acquaintance different than a friend; and a friend different than a closer friend?

The stages between acquaintance, friend and closer friend have to do with commonalities and interests shared. At first, the acquaintance is a person who may have one or two interests (common things) with you. Eventually, this acquaintanceship may lead to the development of a friendship—as the two (or more) of you begin to influence one another and discover more interests and commonalities.

Commonalities shared are discussions shared; discussions exchanged, are deeper friendships made. Thus, the more commonalities one shares with another, the more things there are to talk about. You know how it feels when you first meet someone new and you guy's have nothing to talk about. It's the same thing going on here. It's a strange feeling to feel. This decrease in communication is happening because the two of you have nothing to talk about. Nothing to talk about directly influences your relationship. Unity is formed by some sort of direct relation. This relation could be anything from touch to sex to talking. All of these things are a relation: between you and another person. A relationship is defined as being anything that human beings can relate to with other human beings. For example, if I am staring at a stranger across the room, there is, already, a relationship being built. I am sharing a relationship with her via my eye contact. Our eyes are relating to one another in some way. (She is obviously, by now, rather blushed and starry-eyed!) A relationship soon will develop into a deeper relationship. (You may call this a friendship or something deeper.) As the commonalities increase, communication increases (usually); as the communication increases, time spent together increases; as time spent together increases, intimacy begins to take a more tangible form; as intimacy increase, familiarity increases. Familiarity breeds understanding, and understanding breeds acceptance and mutual love. (Not always. There are exceptions.) Though things may not necessarily go in the order I presented (which is a loose order), deeper friendships are to be found at the end of the relationship spectrum, not at the beginning. This much can be assumed.

All in all, it seems that friendship is the one thing lying beneath human relations. And human relations are all about commonalities and similarities. You work at a hospital because you are a nurse. As a nurse, you don't wake up and go to the auto body shop—the relationship with your own skills and the skills necessary to be at a auto body shop are non-existent. In the end, it's all about relation. If you can't relate to someone, you can't be their friend. (Almost always. Always?)

So what does love and unity have to do with each other? Well, love, for me, in this paper, is merely a deep friendship with sexual relations. It is friendship plus sex. Sex being the one thing that separates erotic love from deep and intimate friendship. Thus, when a man loves a woman, he is taking their intimate friendship to a higher intimacy level: sex. Sex is already a union. Thus, it isn't hard for one to get the idea that sex is unification. If a deep friendship results in sex, we may call this love. (The sort of "love" between a husband and his wife.) Sex is, as I have earlier argued, all about reproduction, pleasure, intimacy and oneness. However, as I have pointed out, sex is almost always directly related to reproduction; and reproduction is the formation of a human being that is a fusion of you and your lover. Thus, my daughter will be merely a reflection of my love for my wife. She will be an *embodiment* of mine and my wife's love. In this sense, sex (and, inevitably, reproduction) is a unity. Holistically speaking, throwing a deep friendship together with marriage, sex and reproduction, one creates the most intimate of human environments. I doubt anything can be more intimate than that. This intimacy is essentially a further development of friendship (which is a form of unity—union of commonalities between two or more humans). This intimacy, which includes sex, leads to the two becoming one flesh. There is, at a later stage, a more pure form of intimate love that includes oneness. This oneness is a unity between two people that runs so deep that nothing can come between this unity. Not even death. Even after death, the unity that "existed" seems to still exist in memories and thoughts of the extant beloved. So powerful is the power of intimate oneness.

By why do humans long for more than just "deep friendship"? Why do we long for sex and intimacy in heterosexual relations? The answer is because we long for a sense of oneness. But why do humans want to feel oneness? And what *is* oneness? Oneness comes into existence just as the distinction between my interests and her interests are blurred; the moment that distinction is overcome—the moment that there really is no true distinction between "me" and "my wife"—is the moment that true, intimate oneness is born. But to what extent does such a union run?

Is such a union realistic? I think that we need to define union in terms of an increase in similarities. For example, I will never, in theory, be indistinguishable from my wife. I will be a male and she will be a female; I will be taller than her and she will be shorter. When people on the street meet us, they will know to "distinguish" between "me" and "my wife." Thus, it is impossible to become "unified" in this most "natural" sense. For those who want to arbitrarily apply union to *everything* are merely distorting the view of union theorists and people like myself. Union, then, must refer to something like "being in synch with another." This sounds like a more appropriate definition. Thus, when rowers are paddling "in union," they are not indistinguishable from each other; rather, they are working together for some common cause. A husband and a wife that are "in union" are working *together*. A relationship that truly features *disunion* is a relationship where the husband and wife work *against* each other. Here is true disunity; where there is no unity. Thus, as a human, I can, twenty years down the road, say that I like the musical band Lifehouse. My unified wife may say that she likes Creed. From a union theory perspective, because our interests are not colliding with one another, we are still "one." I am not set against my wife's views; neither is she set against my tastes. Just because distinction exists doesn't mean that disarray and disunion exist. People who criticize union theorists fail to understand the difference between union and disunion. In fact, my wife and I can work in union by going to two separate concerts together. In a "dis-unified" relationship, the wife and husband, though liking separate bands, may end up going to one concert only (the husband's or the wife's choice). In this case, the husband and wife are working against each other; they are having *either/or decisions*. In a unified relationship, there are no either/or decisions. At least, in theory, they should occur at lower rates.

If one fails to agree with me, one can, at the very least, agree with me that partial union is key to a satisfying relationship. Though I believe in a sort of "absolute union," I can understand the belief in a "partial fusion." Whatever one ends up thinking, friendship, oneness and intimacy all exist as cornerstones in healthy heterosexual relationships. In order for any union to exist between a husband and wife, there must be, first and foremost, the *desire* for the union to exist. A heterosexual couple must strive for union, in a healthy manner: working together. I believe that most humans, if not all, already have the desire to form union. We seek out similarities in others for this very reason: to find some sort of union.

But what happens with autonomy? Does a husband really have a will if his will is no longer extant (since his will is now to be identified with his wife's)? I believe that autonomy still exists. In my view, humans have the desire for friendship and unity. This desire leads to exploring similarities. This further leads to a formation of intimacy. As commonalities increase, fusion occurs between two separate wills. Thus, a husband can say that "we" are pregnant (for both have desired to have sex with one another and have a child); a wife can say that "we" have decided to buy a house. The formation of the "we" already implies a direct unity. Whether others accept this or not, unity is presupposed and encouraged even in our language. (Which is why we have the word "we" in the first place.)

Autonomy (personal independence) still exists in highly fused couples. Fusion, or becoming one, is really already presupposed in the theological idea of the Trinity. According to theologians, God exists in God the Father, Jesus Christ and the Holy Spirit. However, between the Holy Three there exist separate functions and, yet, one function. In a unified couple, there is a "her's," a "mine," and an "ours." There are *three* things that exist within the *one* thing that we call the unified couple. Unity, then, is merely a working together, simplistically speaking. Unity does not imply becoming one, exact thing. It does not mean that my wife will begin looking like me. It does not mean that she will grow a penis like me. Such ideas are as ludicrous as the critics of union theory.

To be "in union" with your wife merely means something as simple as holding her hand and walking down the street together. The keyword is *together*. When two people choose to do things *together*, they are unified. One example will demonstrate autonomy in a unified couple. A wife may want to have sex with her husband. This desire is her desire alone. It is her autonomous will. The husband, too, wants to have sex with his wife. The desire to make love to his wife is his own conscious desire. However, since both of them—*together*—wish to have sex with each other, this can be expressed as "we" would like to have sex. This "we" is the cornerstone and *ipsa verba* of union theory. There exists a unity amongst autonomy. Two human beings come together and work together—with separate identities.

Other Motives for Love

Love does not merely touch bases with unity. Some have viewed love as some sort of "robust concern." According to this view, love is somewhat unconditional and is really aiming at some specific "end" (i.e., the concern for and well-being of the other). Thus, when you "love" someone, you are really just unconditionally caring for his or her well-being. In other words, against the union theory, love isn't really, at the core, about union and friendship, but about concern. This concern is volitional. There is no "we" or intimate union involved (which somewhat dissolves autonomy). In fact, love is autonomous *per se*. Love, then, is a concern for some other being that takes feelings and other emotions into account not. Basically, when you love someone, you love them in spite of whatever feelings occur. The problem with this view is that concern doesn't necessarily have to be "central" to love. In fact, union theory maintains that concern is important—it's just not the means nor ends *per se*. When you are unified with someone, obviously, by becoming one, you care for yourself, herself and "ourself." And why do you care? Because her pleasure becomes your pleasure; her failures become your failures; the air she breathes becomes the life you take in. Moreover, it is presupposed that if you truly love someone, you are friends and care for each other. Why? Because that may result in a loss of fellowship and friendship (which is central to love). This "loss" of friendship makes us humans to be concerned with those with whom we are friends with. For example, as a musician in a band, I am truly concerned about my fellow friends' health and well-being. Why? Because they are my friends, and out of friendship stems concern. Thus, contrary to robust concern theorists, love has friendship as its root, not concern. Concern follows friendship. My band members are friends of mine and we share commonalities together. If I lose my band members, I am, to an extent, losing myself. In such a way does concern arise. It is, in my opinion, hard to be truly concerned for someone with whom you have no relationship with at all. If I don't have a relationship with John Smith, how am I supposed to be concerned for his well-being? On the other hand, if John Smith is dying from cancer, and I don't know him, I may be concerned for him, but this concern arises because there exists a relationship: my views of cancer. I know cancer and so does John Smith. This *relates* us. Thus, his death and/or agony is my concern.

I have sympathy towards him. Had John been infected with some disease of which I had absolutely no knowledge of—i.e., no relation to—I would not have been able to be concerned for John. Had I seen John outside of the hospital and in some other setting—a soccer field, for example—and he told me that he had some sort of "thing" (i.e., a "disease" but without calling it a "disease"—since if he called it a "disease" I would have had an immediate relationship to it, since I would have had an opinion of what it meant to have a disease), I would not have been able to relate whatsoever to John. His words would have been meaningless to me. In turn, I would not be concerned for him (since I wouldn't know what that "thing" was that he had). In order for me to be concerned, I need to know. Knowledge is, generally speaking, gotten from engaging in fellowship. Therefore, it appears that concern presupposes a knowledge and a relationship to the one for whom concern is shown. This concern is secondary to friendship. Thus, friendship lies at the *heart* of love (which is paralleled by concern) and *not* concern. And friendship, as I have defined it, involves, at a later stage, *unity and intimacy*.

Some others, rightly so, view love as valuing. We value those we love; and we love those we value. In other words, if I meet a girl and am attracted to her, this might happen because of my valuing her. But how do I come to that point of "value"? There are, generally speaking, two views regarding how we come to such a state. Some think that our valuing another comes because we *bestow* such a value upon that person. In bestowing this value *upon* another person, we are merely creating an illusion (we bestow kindness on a girl who is, in reality, unkind and greedy). Thus, when we value some other due to our *bestowing* certain views upon that other (which views we love), we are creating some sort of being that doesn't really exist. In common language terms, this is what we call the "love is blind" view. Here, the beloved merely appears to have the values that we have bestowed upon her. Thus, the lover doesn't really love the girl for *who she is* but merely for *who he thinks* (or creates) her to be. For example, let's suppose that I met a pretty girl named Monika at a restaurant. I could, at first, become attracted to her *because* of her looks (predestination?). Such physical attraction can or cannot be controlled. If it cannot be controlled, then love is beyond our controls—which would make the theory of predestination, to some extent, correct. Now, let us suppose, that I find Monika attractive and I make my way towards her. Let us further suppose that Monika is a very cruel and selfish person. Once I meet her, my "love" may be temporarily "blinded." I may spend some time talking to her. After a few dates, I may bestow ideals and morals upon a girl who lacks them. These values that I bestow upon her, I would, inevitably, love. Thus, I would "fall in love" with her. However, the truth is that she has none of those values. I am merely bestowing them upon her. I am creating a perfect Monika girl—whom I love—

but who hardly exists. This is, in summary, a general view of *love as bestowing value*. Nonetheless, at the heart of the matter, love is about *valuing* others (whether it is realistic or illusionary).

On the other hand, we may truly value others who *really have* those values. This is the part where the wise man does not get "blinded" by "love." To use the same analogy again, I may meet Monika at a restaurant and find her attractive. I may then walk towards her and begin talking to her. Upon our initial meeting, I may find her *valuable* in my sight because of the values that she truly (and realistically) has. I would value her for who she is as a person because she really is that person (i.e., I am not projecting my own ideals upon her). I would, thus, fall in love with her and value her as a person—loving her for *who she is*.

At the core of all of this, we find that value is really love. But is it? First, we must define value. Value is, according to my understanding, held in the eyes of the beholder. Every person has different values. Thus, value cannot be universally defined and/or applied. Thus, I think that people value things that they uniquely value themselves. I may value a girl who reads Plato. Why? Because I read Plato. However, for the random Joe down the street, the values that he may be most concerned with may have *nothing* to do with Plato. Values, then, are *person-specific*. Nonetheless, the question still exists: why do we value a person? Well, we value people because they are potential comrades. They are potential friends. In other words, value has everything to do with love's root: intimate friendship. People value those with whom they can have friendships with. Thus, even in valuing others, we are really seeking friendship. This friendship eventually leads to intimacy, unity and sex. Thus, again, at the heart of the issue is the social creature ideal: humans are social creatures who seek friendship and intimacy. This is what lies at the *heart of the matter*. Friendship.

I believe that, at times, it is good to ignore certain trait defects. For example, if I meet Monika and fall in love with her, it would be good for me to ignore certain things that she has. For example, Monika may be an overly patient girl that takes her time all the time. This may make her take her time to an extreme extent—to the point where she takes forever to accomplish anything. Such a "defect" I may live with by ignoring it. In ignoring it, I am, to some extent, *bestowing* values upon her. I am viewing her "good" traits, magnifying them, and denying that any faults exist—I am madly and blindly in love. Benjamin Franklin once remarked, "Keep your eyes wide open before marriage and half shut afterwards." This saying holds true. We need to *appraise* a woman for who she really is (i.e., value her for who she is [appraise her] and not value her by simply *bestowing* values upon her). Once we appraise a woman (and man, for that matter) for who she is, we then may begin to live "blindly." As Albert Schweitzer once famously remarked, "Happiness is nothing more than good health and a bad memory." Truly, we must learn to forgive and *forget*. We should ignore "trait defects" in those who we love. We need to love them for the friendship that we *do* have. In doing so, we will remain friends, lovers and happy.

What is love if viewed as an emotion? If love is to be viewed as an emotion proper, we may begin by saying that love is an emotion if we view love as being an "evaluation" of a specific "target." Thus, when I respond with the love-emotion, I am merely "evaluating" an object (i.e., you) and am responding accordingly. If I see Tully coming towards me, I may spend a couple of seconds evaluating her. Is she angry? Sad? Depressed? Happy? Smexy? Once I evaluate her—let us suppose that she is happy and smexy—I may respond with the love-emotion. I may kiss her or I may hug her. Thus, love—if viewed as an emotion—is a response to a target that I have evaluated. When I am angry (which is considered an emotion), I respond to an object that I have evaluated by slamming fists into a door or by raising my voice. Whatever it is, I would not have been angry in the first place had I not evaluated the target as being offensive and dangerous.

The Motives and Reasons for Love

In everything we do, we must always evaluate our own actions (or inactions, reactions). By evaluating ourselves, we may better understand why we do what we do. In understanding ourselves, we may understand others and why they respond towards us in certain ways. I will offer one example here of a reaction and what the justifications were for that reaction.

Joe is driving down the road. It begins snowing. Joe begins to get angry at the snow. He is upset and begins screaming. Why is Joe angry at the snow? Let us examine the reasons. Joe is driving not just to any ordinary place, he is driving to a date with his wife. Thus, Joe isn't really angry at the snow, he is angry at what the snow is doing to the roads. The snow is making the roads slippery and hard to drive on. Joe thinks that he may be late. But why is Joe concerned with the date with his wife? Well, he wants to get there on time because he knows that's what makes his wife happy—getting to a date on time. Now it seems that Joe isn't really angry at the snow, he is angry at the time delay (which the snow is causing). But why does Joe want to please his wife by showing up on time? Well, maybe he was thinking of making her happy and satisfied. In fact, the more we examine Joe's mind, we begin to see that Joe promised his wife not simply an ordinary evening, but a romantic evening. After the date, Joe was supposed to have sex at a local hotel with his wife. Thus, it seems that Joe isn't really upset about the time delay—he is upset with not pleasing his wife. And, in fact, he isn't really concerned with just his wife's pleasure, but his own also. Had Joe been "mad" at the snow, he would have been mad at it always. The point is that the snow wasn't really the end of the matter—it was merely a means to an end. The end was an intimate night of sex with his wife. Motives. We all have motives. We need to examine them—as they do relate to our love life.

The Irreplaceable Love

I do not think that love is replaceable. Some have viewed love as merely a love of a certain group of properties. In other words, love is really just a group of traits that you love that your spouse has. In theory, then, if someone else were to be found on earth with those very same traits (properties), I would be able to replace my spouse. I do not think that love is replaceable, I will show you why. First of all, if love were merely a collection of properties that a certain person (e.g., your spouse) had, then love would be replaceable. However, love is not simply a love of properties. I do not love my wife merely because of the fact that she cooks Italian dishes and enjoys philosophy and theology. I love my wife because of a million factors. She is a unique individual. She has a certain voice. A certain look in her eyes. A certain facial expression. A very certain physical look to her and a very certain (and highly complex) combination of certain traits. She is most certainly *not* replaceable! Given all of these "certainties," I may add a final objection: my wife is my friend. With her I share a special bond, a special level of intimacy and unity. How could I merely replace her? Would I replace and remake all of the memories with someone else? Would I cross the same rivers twice with the other individual (who dares to replace my wife)? Heraclitus once remarked that "you cannot step into the same river twice." By this, Heraclitus meant that nothing in life can really be relived. Everything is in a state of flux. Had those who believe in the replaceable love considered Heraclitus, they would not have made such rash statements. Nothing in life can I truly relive. In fact, the great philosopher, Søren Kierkegaard, tried to relive the past. He couldn't. He set out to do everything as he had done in the past. It simply didn't work. Even the same street that you've crossed a million times can never be truly the same. It changes; it is in a state of flux. That one time that you walked on it, the street had a temperature of 78 degrees Fahrenheit; now, in your want to relive the past action, the street has a different temperature. On top of that, the people on the street are on different points and are uniquely mixed. The air is no longer the exact same.

My wife cannot be truly replaceable. She shares a certain mix of precise characteristics *and memories*. These memories are truly irreplaceable. If we have children, that done settles it. It's impossible to substitute the woman with whom I've shared both intimate nights with and now with whom I share children. Those who argue that love is replaceable are insane. Mere lunatics who cannot be seriously taken by the realistic population.

The Contract

Let me briefly summarize everything I have said in this paper. Though I have not had the time to argue everything imaginable, I think that I have said enough to stimulate thinking and reflection.

Human existence has friendship at the core. We are social creatures who long for fellowship with one another. This desire for society and social interaction, leads us to have relations with each other and create families. Men marry women to maintain a truly intimate relationship (*present* society) and have children (reproduction and sex) in order to continue this longing for society into the *future*. All in all, friendship and intimacy (a deeper level of friendship) lie at the heart of everything we do. Moreover, in order for relationships to continue (and so society), we must engage in the pursuit of life. This pursuit of life keeps us breathing and living so that we may continue to maintain social relations. All relationships presuppose human life and existence. We exist in order to be social.

Marriage is an institution between man and woman. It serves to promote society, something that all human beings are interested in maintaining. Because we long to be with one another, society is inevitable. In order for society to exist, mating between a male and a female must occur (all other forms of pseudo-marriage must be viewed as destructive to society). Anything that gets in the way of the *pursuit of life* and *reproduction* (different than mere *sex*) is to be contraindicated. Humans exist for fellowship, if something interferes with that, then that must be viewed as an essential evil. Reproduction, as I have earlier stated, implies long-term friendship and commitment (a reproductive relationship between a male and a female). Marriage, then, is an institution that is to be enforced and endorsed by the government (by those social and political philosophers who have the necessary knowledge to make such important decisions). Moreover, marriage must be protected by the government. Society must have laws concerning marriage—and laws require potential punishment. A law without punishment is no law at all.

The Contract is a contract between a husband and a wife who wish to maintain an authorized legal friendship. A friendship that is bound by law and protected by law. Those who engage in such marriages (via The Contract) must remain together to protect innocent children. Divorce must be allowed on thorough and strict grounds. However, divorce must never be encouraged. (Unless the children, who are protected by The Contract, are at risk for harm.) Education must inevitably be promoted regarding the seriousness and need of heterosexual marriage. Only those who have been adequately educated, who have tasted the waters of understanding, may partake in legal marriage. Those who get "married" without reading the fine print are creating unnecessary potentials for divorce.

Love, as I have defined it, is to be greatly promoted. Love and intimacy are very important for healthy marriages. The Contract, though strict, only seeks to promote a love that is long-term and beneficial (not merely to the couple, for the children as well). The Contract seeks to benefit not merely the couple (which it hopes may remain in love, friendship and unity) but also the potential children from the heterosexual union. The Contract, in short, seeks to promote overall and holistic happiness. Some fathers may have to remain bound by the contract in a lukewarm marriage to raise children. The Contract presupposes sacrifice. And love is sacrifice.